# THE LONGER LENT

## SEPTUAGESIMA TO EASTER

# THE LONGER LENT

## SEPTUAGESIMA TO EASTER

### FOURTEEN ADDRESSES

INCLUDING TWO FOR EASTER DAY AND ONE FOR THE
FEAST OF S. MATTHIAS

BY THE

# REV. VIVIAN R. LENNARD, M.A.

*Rector of Lower Heyford (Oxon)*

AUTHOR OF "WOMAN, HER POWER AND INFLUENCE,"
"HARVEST-TIDE," "PASSIONTIDE AND EASTER," ETC.

London
SKEFFINGTON & SON
34, SOUTHAMPTON STREET, STRAND, W.C.
1911

# PREFACE.

THE Lectionary, in its selected Sunday readings, from the Books of Genesis and Exodus, appointed for this season, suggests that during the longer Lent, from Septuagesima to Easter, side lessons of example or of warning, drawn from the Old Testament, may well be allowed a place (if a secondary one) in our scheme of Lenten study.

The present volume is a humble attempt to give expression to this suggestion.

S. Chrysostom tells us that the Book of Genesis was always read during Lent. And though the special lessons for Sundays were chosen by our Reformers, yet they adhered to this general principle until we reach the fifth Sunday, when the story of the Exodus is commenced.

Their selection shows the gradual separation of the chosen race, in the severance of Noah from the men of the old world, of Abraham from his kindred, and of Jacob from Esau. Thus in these three names, Noah, Abraham, Jacob, we have the exodus which preceded that under Moses, and prepared for that under Christ.

There is little doubt that the elucidation of this principle was a primary object with the compilers of the Lectionary in their choice of Genesis and the opening chapters of Exodus, as suitable readings for this season; for it is a noticeable feature of the history, that from the time of the first temptation, the law of conflict and the law of separation are exemplified at every step.

Thus we see the wheat gradually sifted from the chaff, the good consummated through trial, and the victory won through sacrifice.

Throughout these early records, the discipline of pain (symbolized in the initial rite of the Patriarchal Church, as the instrument of a moral and spiritual separation) appears again and again in the history, written in characters of blood.

In the trial of Abraham, the temptations of Lot and of Joseph, we have varied illustrations of the power of evil, and the inevitable conflict which man must wage with sin; while in the martyrdom of Abel, and the sacrifice of Isaac, we have touching memorials which point onwards to the fulfilment of all sacrifice, in the one Eternal Offering of the "Lamb slain from the foundation of the world."

It goes without saying that the indifferent and

irreligious usually pay but little heed to the season of Lent. Hence it is to religious people that its appeals are made. And to them, both its warnings and invitations are more particularly addressed. For this reason, the author has dwelt with special emphasis upon the characters of Eli and Lot (both good but weak men), as pointing lessons of warning and rebuke to good or religious people.

V. R. L.

# CONTENTS.

# THE LONGER LENT.

## I.

## SEPTUAGESIMA SUNDAY.

### The Past and the Future.

GENESIS xvi. 8,

"Whence camest thou?" and "Whither wilt thou go?"

HERE are two questions, a question of our past, and a question of our future.

In Scripture history, the question, "Whence comest thou?" has always been one of sad significance.

It was first put to Hagar, the Egyptian slave-girl, as she fled from her mistress Sarai, into the wilderness of Shur, towards the land of her nativity.

Hagar, like other slaves, had been harshly treated, though hers was not a case of grievous wrong. There were faults on her own side as well as on that of her mistress. And so, when she fled from her home and duty, it pleased God to send His angel to the misguided girl, stopping the runaway slave with the question of the text, " Hagar, whence camest thou, and whither wilt thou go ? "

Again, the question is that with which the Prophet Elisha met Gehazi, as he returned from his secret interview with Naaman, the Syrian general.

Just when he seemed to have made his fortune, and his avaricious hopes were being realised, Elisha met him with the question, " Whence comest thou, Gehazi ? " and since it called forth no timely repentance, but only an added lie intended to cloak his fault, that question served to introduce the terrible sentence which followed, " The leprosy therefore of Naaman shall cleave unto thee, and unto thy seed for ever."    And he, who might have been a prophet's successor, went out from Elisha's presence "a leper as white as snow," destined only to be the father of a miserable race, whom his own guilt had cursed.

Then there was Jonah, trying to do the impossible, flying from the presence of Jehovah, whom even the grave refused to receive, and the sea to retain ; trying to do what every man tries to, when he sins against light and conscience, getting away from God for awhile, only to find Him more terribly present in the future; sleeping through the storm, which combatted his wayward policy; directing the suspicions of the terrified seamen towards the careless stranger who voyaged with them, who, when they had cast lots for whose cause the storm was sent, and the lot fell upon Jonah, gathered round him with eager, hurried questions, of which the text is one, "Whence comest thou?"

It was this very question which elicited from Satan himself the answer, "I come from going to and fro in the earth, and from walking up and down in it"; and it was this same question (with only a trifling alteration) that our Saviour put to the traitor Judas, as he approached at the head of a band of conspirators, to give them the betrayer's token, "Comrade, wherefore art thou come?"

This question of the past, then, has been one of painful discovery; yet it is none the less our duty to put it faithfully to ourselves.

And first, as regards our race.

The question, "Whence comest thou?" carries our minds back to man as he was made in the beginning when, fresh from the hands of the Creator, God looked upon all His work, "And behold it was very good." Alas! from what a height has man fallen, and how long has he grovelled (like the serpent which deceived him) in the dust. Hence it follow that "Even an Aristotle is but the ruins of an Adam."

It has been said with regard to the westward emigration of the race, and in memory of that pleasant East, where man had his lofty origin and primeval home, "That our sad journey is ever further from the East." We thank God this is not true. We believe in human progress, in a restoration of our fallen race, but fallen that race undeniably is, and it is well sometimes to look back so far as the days of man's innocence, to see how we were made, and wherefore we were created.

Again, with respect to our nearer ancestry. Blue blood and gentle birth are things not to be despised, while a godly parentage is even to be preferred.

To have had ancestors whose words and deeds speak to us from the dust, whose examples are still present with us, to bid us follow them as they followed Christ, is a gift much to be desired.

But if such is not our happy lot, if the memory of our forefathers is only a thought to trouble us, if our ancestors were remarkable only for their weakness or their shame, still, there are lessons of humiliation and warning to be learned from the past. Shall *we* be

careless and self-confident where others have
fallen ?

Is that step, or that habit, less dangerous
for us than for our fathers ?

We have read its consequences over and
over again in their biographies ; should not
that teach us to avoid the slide upon which
they missed their footing ?

But the most important application of the
text still remains.

The question of our individual past, " Whence
comest thou ? "

We ourselves are the products of the past.
What we are to-day is the direct consequence
of what we were yesterday. It is with individuals
as with the race ; we see more of what man
has made of himself than of what God
made him. Already we have entered into the
labours of former years.

Sowing time is not ended, yet our reaping
has begun ; and the full or meagre harvest of
the present is the fruit of the past. " The child
is father of the man." Few of us, I suspect,
can look back upon life without regrets.
Memory will recall many things painful and
humiliating. Happy are they, who, in the face
of this humiliation, can also look back upon
sin forsaken and repented of, upon a definite

purpose formed long ago, upon faith exercised, and prayer answered, upon a sustained life, and steps supported by a covenant God. But if it should be otherwise, if there is nothing definite and satisfactory to look back upon, if the answer to the question, " Whence comest thou ? " is only from sin to sin, from the ignorance of childhood, to the folly of youth, and on to the riper wickedness of maturer years, from omission to commission, from negligence to unbelief, from secret desire to open impiety, still, for every crushed and humbled soul, there is a "turn again, Whittington," in the opportunities of this life, and the promises of Holy Scripture.

Your probation is still continued. For you the sun rises and shines. For you the earth brings forth and bears. For you Christ died. God Himself loves you, why should you despair ? "

But whatever our religious attainments may be, the past is deserving of a careful review.

It is the explanation of what we are.

It suggests much that in the future we may expect, and should prepare for.

It is the history of your individual weaknesses, and God's dealings with you ; study it.

But there is also the question of our future : " Whither wilt thou go ? "

Have you ever dared to look the future full

in the face? To interrogate the unknown possibilities beyond the grave? To question that ominous silence, and in no spirit of idle curiosity, but in that of honest inquiry, to lift the awful veil, and enter the dark chamber of mystery, and wring from the Oracle's own lips something of your destiny?

Believe me, there are many who never do this, who shun serious inquiry altogether.

And there is a sense in which it is wrong to be curious about the future, and to speculate of things hidden from us.

But this is a very different thing from living as if we had no future : from letting the narrow present bound both our thoughts and desires.

It is our duty to look ahead, to judge, so far as we can, the chances and possibilities of life, for which we are in a measure accountable, and to prepare ourselves for them.

And we may be all sure enough of one thing, that our future will be the resultant of the past ; that it will take its shape and colour from what has gone before.

But to enter somewhat more into detail.

In the words, "Whither goest thou?" three questions are involved or implied: a question of duty, of desire, and of choice.

What *should* you do? What *would* you do? What *will* you do?

And first, the question of duty. Have you made sure of that? Do you really know your duty? Are you certain about the direction in which you ought to go? I will not ask what do you *feel* about religion, but I ask what do you *know*? What are your convictions?

Next, the question of desire. What *would* you do? If all secondary motives of fear or policy were dismissed, where would inclination lead? Do the "eyes look right on" and the "eyelids look straight before them"? Do you, like Daniel, pray always "toward Jerusalem"? Can you, with David, say, "My soul longeth, yea, even fainteth, for the courts of the Lord: my heart and my flesh crieth out for the living God"?

Lastly, the question of choice. What *will* you do? All depends upon this. You may know your duty, and even desire to do it, but the result will depend upon the final choice.

I do not mean that your destiny rests upon a single decision, though that may be very important, for life is made up of decisions, of choices, each of which goes to form another. But I do say, that upon the resultant decision, which is the sum of all these decisions, your destiny depends.

It is quite true that we cannot take up the

Book of Fate and read our part therein, and yet it is equally true that faith need have no fears about the future.

When S. Paul said, "I know whom I have believed, and am persuaded that He is able to keep that which I have committed unto Him against that day," the question of his destiny was practically settled.

Our destiny is mercifully hidden from us, but our duty is not hidden from us, and a man's destiny depends upon his decisions respecting duty. We are the arbiters of our destiny, then, not by the possession of unaided power, but through the gift of a free choice.

Once, at least, in a life-time, the question of the text comes to each of us as it came to Hagar, when the angel found her wandering in the wilderness of Shur, between Mamre and Egypt.

Sometimes the question comes to us in the pursuit of wealth, or some other fleeting good, in the effort to catch at some deluding shadow which the hand cannot grasp, because it is a shadow, or in the weariness which is the invariable reward of undedicated toil and unsanctified ambition.

Again and again those words have pursued us, " Whither wilt thou go ? "

Or it may be that we have been living a very

careless and unthinking life, though not an immoral one.

We have sought our own ease, and indulged every fancy: playing at life, rather than living. We have taken things just as they came, and never seriously set ourselves to inquire what was our duty and vocation: and we have been contented with this sort of existence, after a fashion, putting conscience aside and laughing away all scruples, hushing to sleep each graver thought, until the candle of desire went out and left us alone in the darkness; and then, for very weariness, we have asked the question we ought to have asked so long before, Whither am I going?

Or, we have wandered over the dreary wastes of religious speculation until the question has forced itself upon us, to what is this leading me? Already I have forfeited peace and assurance. These views have long since taken the Bible from me. Prayer is presumption, and worship folly. Where will all this end? Now that the ship has slipped her moorings, and is out in the wide waters, with no kindly stars above, and no friendly chart within, whither, oh! whither, shall she go?

Or, we have been pulled sharply up, in the soft and easy descent of vice, as the feet were gliding swiftly down the grassy slope towards the precipice below.

Sin had followed sin until a habit was formed, and the habit had become a passion, and the passion delirium, until a sudden illness or some unexpected deliverance arrested our progress; the angel stopped and talked with us, and once more the question was put, "Whither wilt thou go?"

Oh! my friends, as you stand to-day, with the power of a free choice in your hand, with life before you, and each point of the compass open for your selection, East, West, North, and South, "Choose you this day whom ye will serve."

Alas! what little things are allowed to influence our choice. When once the desire is enlisted, it needs but a trifling temptation to answer the momentous question for us.

It is said that the beautiful Priory of Bolton, in Yorkshire, was founded by a sorrowing mother in memory of her only son, who, one day while out hunting with a greyhound, had reached a certain point in the River Wharfe called the "Strid," where its waters rush between two projections of rock which nearly meet. A hundred times before the youth had safely leapt the "Strid." But now, as he sprang forward, the dog in the leash suddenly hung back, and both were precipitated into the torrent below and were drowned.

It is an apt illustration how some minor choice

is allowed to decide for us our destiny. How some trifling omission in duty, some fond indulgence steadily persisted in (the weekly revel or occasional debauch, a foolish lover or a wicked companion) a dog, or something else, is enough to pull us down.

And now I must leave this question with you. Hide it in your memories, consider it with respect to two things—God and sin. Are you striving to forsake sin, or are you cherishing it? Will you fly from God, or to God?

Will you try again that fruitless endeavour, which has been tried so often, and failed so completely, the cowardly endeavour of a cringing, guilty soul to hide itself from God; like Adam, to get away from the Voice calling you, by hiding amongst the trees of the garden, vainly seeking to cover a conscious nakedness by some refuge of lies.

Like Jonah, fleeing to Tarshish, going down to Joppa, taking ship, going down into the hold, falling asleep, going down into the sea, entering the whale, down, down, down, and even there, in the lowest deep, unable to rid yourself of the Divine presence. Adam, Jonah, and thousands besides them, have tried that plan and failed. Suppose you try another way. "Draw nigh to God, and He will draw nigh to you." Say with holy Job, " I would seek unto God, and unto God would I commit my cause." The Saviour is asking *vou*, as once He asked the disciples, " Will ye also go away ? " Has your heart yet learned the disciples' answer ? " Lord, to whom shall we go ? Thou hast the words of Eternal Life ? "

## II.

## SEXAGESIMA SUNDAY.

## Individual Responsibility.

GENESIS iii. 9.
"Where art thou?"

THE Old Testament continually represents the Almighty as addressing Himself to man.

In the persons of Adam, Cain, Abraham, Moses, and others who succeeded them, we hear the Divine Voice speaking to him individually, appealing to his inner consciousness, calling him by name, in order to instruct, admonish, or console.

These communications were not infrequently couched in the form of questions.

The first of these recorded in Holy Scripture is that given in the text, "Where art thou?" It was addressed to Adam, in the Garden of Eden, after his temptation and fall.

The second of these Divine questions, as they occur in history, is one addressed to Cain, "Where is Abel thy brother?" These two questions cover the whole range of human responsibility.

"Where art thou?" points to the position of man as a created being, formed for the knowledge and worship of God; points also to his condition as a fallen being, a sinner, needing restoration and forgiveness.

On the other hand, the question, "Where is Abel thy brother?" suggests that man is a social being, with duties outside and independent of himself, beyond his own interests, his own needs and salvation.

Together they show that human responsibility is of two kinds, that religion has two aspects, the individual and the corporate, the spiritual and the natural; for all our obligations resolve themselves into two simple departments of feeling and action, duty to God and duty to our neighbour.

And in the early chapters of the world's history as in the opening days of our individual life, these are expressed in their most elementary form, "Where art thou?" "Where is Abel thy brother?"

Take the first of these, the question addressed

to Adam, which stands on the first page of
man's biography, and refers fo human responsibility in its more primary aspect, the question,
"Where art thou?" Where art thou in relation to thy Maker? What honour or dis-
honour hast thou done to the Divine Image
which is hidden in thy soul, which is stamped
upon thy features and reflected in thy Godlike
mind and intellect?

Where art thou in relation to the partner
and companion who stands at thy side, the
divinely appointed helpmeet, whom God has
chosen to be thy joy and solace on earth?
Where art thou in relation to that coming race,
which shall one day people the world and bless
or curse it with their virtues or their crimes?

Where art thou in thy relation to the great
mystery of knowledge, and in thy attitude
towards the still greater mystery of evil, the full
significance of which is as yet hidden from
thee?

Such was the question addressed to Adam as
he vainly endeavoured to conceal himself from
the presence and voice of the questioner,
amongst the trees of the garden, "Where art
thou?"

My brothers! The times are changed. The
world has grown older since this question

was first asked. But man is still the same. His circumstances and surroundings have altered. In his environment it might seem, indeed, that he is another being altogether, another creature, so different are the conditions of his life. But in essentials he is still the same ; and this Divine question, asked so many centuries ago, is to-day the all-important question for man.

It is a question which each one of us must answer now or in the day of final appeal.

What is our relation to God? How do we stand in His sight? What is our relation to knowledge, and to all the gifts and oppor-tunities of life ? What is our attitude towards evil? Adam, "Where art thou ? "

My brothers, this question of our relation to God underlies all other questions of import-ance. It confronts us at every crisis of our changeful life. " Where art thou? "

It will meet us in the solemn hour of death, and there press for an answer when it cannot be denied.

The question, as regards our worldly state and condition, has a keen interest for most of us, while in its deeper aspects it is too often left unasked or unanswered. In this lower sense it is still urged with eager solicitude, Where am I ?

What is my position in society? How do I stand in the eyes of others?

Now we know where man stands in the order of creation. The answer is the same whether we accept the theory of evolution or not. He is at the head of the series. All life ministers to his life. Nature acknowledges him as master and lord. We know where he stands in the history of Redemption. His title and position are manifested in an ever ascending order of dignity and glory, in the Incarnation, the Resurrection, and Ascension, of the Son of Man.

But is this felt and recognised by ourselves individually? Are we living and acting in harmony with the great truths which we acknowledge and confess, or are we standing outside the circle of their influence and attraction, like a planet that has forsaken its orbit and has no relation whatever to its system, or like a false note which has no connection with the chord in which it is sounding? These questions demand an answer, and that answer must be given by us individually. It is not enough that we should act as do others, or follow where they lead; for it is as individuals that God deals with us, both in Creation and Redemption; and we ought to cherish as a most sacred gift the power of thinking and

acting for ourselves ; for we cannot part with
our individuality.   All there is in us of strength
or goodness is bound up with this which fixes
our identity and makes us responsible beings.

In the words of the late Bishop Creighton,
" Men are not born in the mass nor educated in
the mass, they are born into this world one by
one, and one by one they live and pass out of
this world into another."

Nowhere are the duties of man as a social
being more strongly enforced than in the Old
and New Testaments ; yet nowhere is religion
set forth more uncompromisingly as a claim
upon the individual man—" Where art thou ? "

Without this sense of individuality there can be
no strength of impulse and no warmth of enthusiasm.   For there is no sense of responsibility
except such as springs from the recognition of
our own  personal  relation  towards  God.   To
weaken this is to enfeeble every motive which
is derived from it.   We must regard any en-
croachment upon this, therefore, as an attack
upon the citadel of our life.

You may think the matter unimportant, but
nothing is unimportant that weakens our sense
of responsibility.   " Where art thou ? " stands
in the forefront of human history as the first
question addressed by God to man ; and it has

still a message to us, in the appeal which it
makes to our individuality, in which it seems to
warn us, in these changed times, against the
domination of fashion, and bids us resist above
all things that state of dependency which is
content to be merged in a crowd, and is satisfied
if only it may share the spirit, the aspirations,
and the fate of the great bulk of mankind.

To be entirely maleable to the influences of
society, so that the world moulds *us* and not *we*
the world, is to forfeit, most distinctly, the very
purpose for which God made us to differ one
from another. Yet this is one of the dangers to
which all men are exposed, especially those
whose lot is cast in the strenuous and competi-
tive life of a great city. The domination of
society is such that men are more and more
under the influence of that vast corporation in
which they live and work and have their daily
interests ; and there is positive danger lest they
should be absorbed, and their individuality lost,
in so mighty a whole.

Here and there a great personality rises out
of this surging ocean, this whirlpool of rival
claims and interests, to command our admiration
or respect. But ordinary men are crushed and
borne down in the struggle. Their power of
resistance is unequal to the accumulated forces

to which they find themselves exposed. Content to follow where others lead, they read the same books, acquire the same habits and opinions, and their independence being thus undermined, they gradually lose the power ot thinking and acting for themselves. Hence, not only their intellectual power but their moral sense is weakened, and their personal force diminished, by the combined action of other agencies and other wills.

This is one danger of the times. But as a reaction from this, there is another, in the direction of free thought and unrestricted inquiry, which is even more serious. How many, alas! stand isolated and detached from any fixed centre of hope or belief. Men whose every step declares them lost to all spiritual attractions, groping "in the noonday as in the night," when every decision of the past is questioned or denied, when the most elemental truths are thrown into the crucible of free speculation, and man, both as regards his being and his actions, his purpose in life, and his destiny, is regarded only as a curious problem, interesting indeed, but insoluble.

Surely it is a gloomy outlook. To stand on this earth as the acknowledged head of creation,

C

as part of a system in which each single department and feature demands a personal God and Father as its natural and inevitable explanation; to occupy this position, I say, and yet possess no settled convictions with respect to either our part or destiny in this wondrous system.

Sad it is for any man when, to that old question, "Where art thou?" he can return but a negative answer, expressive of doubt.

Thus, there was never, perhaps, a time when it was more necessary to press upon the individual conscience this question, especially with regard to man's relation to the great Father his belief in a Divine Revelation, and his hope in the Eternal Sacrifice, "Where art thou?"

We have one answer to the question before us in the picture given us in the chapter from which the text is taken, of the man driven forth from Eden, carrying with him into exile an acute sense of self-condemnation and estrangement from his Maker. It represents what is still a matter of common experience. The portrait is still true, whenever a man forfeits innocence and eschews the things which are right. In the case of Adam and his partner in exile, the entrance of sin had altered their entire relation, both to God and to the world around them. Their future was all changed. Together they had sinned, together they had left that bright home of innocence and joy.

It is the one redeeming thought in the dark story of the first transgression and its far-reaching consequences, this picture of wedded life, of man's dual lot, the sorrowing pair going forth in toil and struggle to face together the hardships which their own folly had bequeathed.

This is one answer.

Man is a fugitive and a wanderer, exiled, estranged, cut off from those close and tender relations in which he once stood to the great Father of mankind. But all this may be reversed, for our relation may be again that of children in the home, and of sons restored to their father, who are once more partakers in all the privileges of sonship.

David describes this happy renewal in the fortieth Psalm. He speaks of the discovery which a penitent soul makes of its own misery and alienation, and of its subsequent return. His words are : " He brought me up also out of an horrible pit, out of the miry clay, and set my feet upon a rock, and established my goings." Here is a description of what the Psalmist knew right well, "the pit," "the horrible pit." Like Adam, he had sunk. His feet had left the hard and solid rock. He had trodden the slippery path of evil, and deliberately chosen the downward course. His goings were clogged, like the steps of a man who walks through miry clay; for a human soul had fallen, and the shadow of guilt was resting upon it. But a great change had come over the subject of these experiences. The Psalmist had made a startling discovery. He had answered the question addressed to his conscience and higher nature, and having recognised the guilt and danger of his position, had confessed his sin and grasped the hand stretched out for his help. Thus his spiritual nature was stirred, his moral being had reasserted itself, and having welcomed the Divine aid, his soul had gone forth to meet it, and the penitent's restoration was the result.

But in asking yourself this question of the text, apply it to your work, your home, your church, and your religion. "Where art thou?"

Some of you may remember Archbishop Benson, in this connection, alluding to one of Ruskin's most famous passages about Art. "Speaking of the old builders of the cathedrals he says, how is it that architecture is so beautiful. His answer is, 'that it is because the men's souls were in it.' For he says, 'architecture cannot be carried to perfection except

by *good* men,' and that the time will come
when people will say, not 'what manner of
stones are here, but what manner of men,'
because they will read the men's hearts in
the stone."

Well! it is so with our own work. In its
thoroughness or its incapacity, its heartiness
or its languor, it is a part of ourselves. The
question, "Where art thou?" What art thou?
will have to be answered in our work.

Again, as regards your home. Is it like the
home at Bethany, or the house of Mary, the
mother of John Mark? Does the voice of
prayer ascend from it? Are bad words
silenced and bad books prohibited? Or is the
Bible hidden away in a corner as if it were
the only thing of which you were ashamed?
In your parental relations and attitude towards
your children are you careful that nothing shall
obtrude itself which could weaken their father's
influence or lower him in the eyes of those who
should see in him only what they can love and
honour? Is it a haven of rest to the weary
toiler, the abode of comfort and contentment,
because it is the home of industry and thrift, of
sobriety and peace, of cheerfulness and good-
will? In your home life, "Where art thou?"

Again, as regards your church. How many

who live under its shadow, or within sound of its bells, never listen to their tuneful, pleading message! Thousands of the very poor in our large towns, to whom the services of God's House would bring help and consolation, never enter it, except, it may be, at a midnight service on New Year's Eve. It is little better in the country. Even among those who are neither sceptical nor irreligious, in every class of society, there are men whose church-goings during the twelve months of the year might be counted on the five fingers of one hand.

Let me then, in relation to the privileges of your parish church, ask you once more the question, " Where art thou? "

Lastly, as regards your religion. In what does it consist? Are you any the better for it? The religion of many consists in nothing more than certain vague sentiments connected with death and judgment. A few chance sayings, picked up here and there, and loosely strung together, constitute their only creed. Yet this is but a poor ark for the saving of a human soul. Such a belief has far less consistency than that of a devout Mahomedan. It is scanty, indeed, compared with the belief of Abraham, Moses, or the old Jews.

What our religion should be is nearness to

God through Jesus Christ.  A personal knowledge of Christ.  Conscious love for Him as He
is revealed to us in Holy Scripture.  Frequent
communion with Jesus our Saviour.  The soul
taking Him as its friend in life, its safeguard in
temptation, its hope in death.  There was no
doubt of this in the case of the disciples;
"Where art thou?" was an answered question
with them.  "Lord, to whom shall we go?"
they asked, "Thou hast the words of eternal
life."

# III.

## QUINQUAGESIMA SUNDAY.

### Social Obligations.

GENESIS iv. 9.

" Where is Abel thy brother ?"

THE question before us was addressed by God Himself to the first-born son of Adam, after the rejection of his sacrifice, when in moody indignation and jealous wrath he had risen and slain his brother.

In one guilty act the shedder of blood had sundered that which God had joined together, and destroyed at once the bond of brotherhood and the unity of man.

Thus, strife entered the home and division the family. The great breach had been made. Henceforth, man must expect to wrestle with his neighbour. After this, what might not follow ?

Division of language, division of aim, division of thought.

To ourselves, all this is sadly familiar. It is an old story, the strife of nations, of parties, of Churches, separation of interest and of feeling, Society continually repeating the fratricide of Cain, following the world's motto, " Everyone for himself."

But against this law of might against right, this " gospel of selfishness " as it has been called, amid all the changed conditions of our earthly lot, we hear in the city, the church, the home, the Divine Voice repeating as before the old question, " Where is Abel thy brother? " There is no getting away from this question. Our duties to our fellows are as real as our duties to God, and the former spring out of the latter. Because God is our Father, therefore man is our brother, and all the relationships of life become sacred things, for our contact with them is not accidental, it is essential to our life on earth. When we are born we are born with parents, relations, companions; and though the variety and complexity of these relations will change with the structure of society, yet the fact itself remains. We are social beings with duties and responsibilities one towards another, and our duty in life is not only to protect our own faith and conscience from injury,

but also to infuse into those with whom we are
brought in contact something of our own energy
and life.

Say then to yourself, " I have no right, as a
responsible being, to be a mere cypher in this
vast array of figures, which constitutes collective
man.    I have, it is true, to preserve my own
integrity of character, but I am also bound to
avoid all selfish isolation from my neighbours."
There is much beautiful teaching in that word
"neighbour."    It means the person who is *near*
to us ; to whom anything brings us into close and
intimate relation—our work, our school, our
church.    These all associate us with some to
whom otherwise we should remain strangers.    Our
Lord's incomparable story of the Good Samaritan
has taught us that not only he who lives next
door, but he whom circumstance has thrown in
our way, anyone, in fact, whose path in life
intersects ours, is our neighbour.    Relatives have
naturally the first claim ; and few of us have
any idea how much more numerous our actual
relatives are than we might suppose.    Blackstone,
the great legal commentator, gives Tables of
Consanguinity, in which it is shown that, on the
lowest computation, a man's actual kindred, within
the sixth degree, number over a thousand, and,
within the tenth degree, over a quarter of a million.

Hence, many whom we meet as casual acquaint-
ances, many whom we pass and repass on the
broad thoroughfare of life as having no apparent
connection with us, are in truth our own blood
relations. And to go a little further still. If, as
we believe, we are descended from a common
ancestry, then mankind is our brother; for as the
apostle declares, " God hath made of one blood
all nations of men for to dwell on all the face of
the earth."

It is on this basis of universal obligation,
springing out of our common humanity, that
Christ sketched His inimitable story of the Good
Samaritan, and taught that the tie of brotherhood
should be recognised and strengthened by the
bond of love.

Man is perpetually raising barriers between
himself and others, and hedging himself about
with selfish and exclusive interests, social barriers,
educational barriers, religious barriers.

Now the New Testament, as I read it, does
not aim at the annihilation of social distinctions,
but always recognises and upholds them. Properly considered, they form the truest bond of
union between man and man. For the ideal union
is surely not absolute equality in circumstances or
position, but the union of a body in which each
member has independence of office and action,

coupled with mutual obligations, and cemented by common aims and interests;—a union which embodies these two principles, oneness of purpose, with diversity of operation.

But too often we allow trivial and arbitrary distinctions to suppress and override the initial claims of our common relationship as men and Christians. It was in reference to this that our Lord uttered those remarkable words, "But be not ye called Rabbi." The saying cannot be regarded as intended to weaken the authority of teachers, parents, or rulers, but only to ensure that no arbitrary and assumed distinction should be allowed to obliterate and extinguish those deeper relationships which exist in nature and in Christ.

The tendency of Christianity is perpetually to combat human selfishness and bind us one to another, so as to make all men kin. We see its fruits in the abolition of slavery, the propagation of missions, the recognition of the equality of the sexes, and the protection of the poor and weak, together with the elevation in the tone of public opinion, which now obtains, on the subject of our duty to our neighbour. Even the little conventions of society, which are sometimes hollow and super-ficial, are nevertheless, in this respect, imitations of the law of Christ, in so far that they are generally based upon the claims of others to our respect and consideration. That these claims are real, and have a right to be heard, is proved by the fact that the association of a common danger or a common joy is usually sufficient to call forth in us sentiments of kindness and affection. For there is an instinct of relationship in man, which only needs some fitting occasion to break down interposing barriers, and make us own and feel our common brotherhood.

The primary cause of division between men and classes is selfishness—a vice which takes all manner of shapes, and is a never failing source of alienation and discord. How sad it is to think that the things which ought to bind us most closely to one another are often themselves the causes of further separation ! For example, money should be a bond of union between the wealthy man and his poorer neighbour. Whereas, it is frequently the very reverse of this. In the same way the common business should be a tie of mutual knowledge and interest between members of the same trade or profession, instead of which we know that very often it only serves to sever men from each other. The rival shopkeeper or trades-man, the man who, in a sense, is most your neighbour, becomes your foe, through the dis-integrating power of a fierce and selfish competition. Alas! how blind we are to the mutual obligations which exist between class and class, and to the many and varied links which are intended to unite men to their fellows.

It needs but a little consideration to show that the most solemn and tender associations cluster round the common acts of our daily life. The food we eat, the clothes we wear, the books we read, all the varied comforts we enjoy, are connected with human life and human suffering, because they are the products of human labour. Every blessing we receive imposes a burden of toil or care on someone. We purchase our enjoyments in the sweat of another's face. Thus each day we live adds to the ever-increasing debt we owe our brother. For us the hard hands of toil have laboured. For us our fellows have braved the perils of the sea, and the dangers of the mine. Not our kinsfolk only, but men of other clime and alien speech have contributed their little to make us happy.

Towards this end, young and old, rich and poor, have united in the manifold labours of the world, the results of which, through the complex relations of modern times, are enjoyed by each of us. For God has bound up our interests in the bundle of life with those of our brother. Man cannot be independent of man. Our Maker has inseparably linked us together in bonds of closest union, for no man "liveth to himself." All the good we enjoy from the cradle to the grave, comes to us through human instrumentality. And yet we ignore our fellows, and glory in the narrow boast, "I owe no man anything." My brothers! it is not true. Could we but see the long line of busy workers, who have toiled through successive years to supply the artificial wants which we claim during the short hours of a single day, we should see before us a mighty army of living and dead, a host of men whose names are unknown, or long since forgotten, whose thought and service is profiting us now. They laboured, and we have "entered into their labours." Take the case of any common trade. How many little inventions which advantage the modern workman, and ease the strain of body or mind, are due to the thought, and patience, and self-denial of former generations; to men who were often martyrs to their own genius, and to the stupidity and short-sightedness of their compeers. They rise up before us a mighty army, regiment upon regiment, to claim from us the just tribute of a neighbour's gratitude.

My brothers! it is no fancy picture, but a statement of sober fact. For it is a *real* debt we owe mankind, even the debt of love.

One object of the "simple life" is to "have to

give to him that needeth." Let us not lose sight of this.

There is a great awakening of public interest in the matter of social claims and social duties. Our duty to our neighbour is pressed upon us from platform and pulpit with ever-increasing earnestness. The old parable of the Good Samaritan is printed in fresh type and new setting, and is being rehearsed in tavern and office, in labour bureau and committee room, as the one subject of primary interest and importance. Some of us doubt or dislike the methods of action suggested in many quarters. We think them visionary, even predatory, unwise, and unjust. But whatever methods coming generations may decide to adopt, we should be at one as to the end before us, which should ever be kept in view, viz., the amelioration of the condition of the poor. Let us not, in our differences of opinion, lose sight of the main principle, the eradication or diminution of social evils, and the indemnification of social wrongs.

But you may say, "If I am to help others, how shall I do it?" Shall I not want an elaborated sphere of action? Shall I not require to leave my home and my ordinary work in order that I may give myself to this?" Nothing of the kind. In the words of the late Professor Drummond, "Do you ask, 'How am I to begin'? Begin as

Christ did. First He looked at the city, then He wept over it, then He died for it. Or do you ask, 'Where am I to begin'? Begin where you are. Make that one corner, room, house, office, as like heaven as you can. By far the greatest thing a man can do for the place he lives in is to be a good man. Simply to live there as a good man, as a Christian man of action and sympathy. It is goodness that tells, goodness first and last. Good men, even with small views, are immeasurably more important to the world than small men with great views."

The ordinary relations of life are the natural lines upon which the Creator intended us to work out our mission to our fellow-men. We have not to seek for ourselves new methods of doing our duty. We have not to create opportunities of usefulness. They lie ready to our hand, in the ordinary relations of life. They are within easy reach, for the gift of influence flows most readily in these natural lines of God's appointment. Take friendship, for example. What a power it is, from our earliest to our latest days. As a modern writer says, " Companionships make us." " Every-one who takes a half-mile walk with us lays something on the wall of our life." Margaret Fuller said that " All the good she had ever done had been done by calling on every nature for its highest." "If the home duties," said Confucius "are well performed, what need is there to go afar to offer sacrifice?" Have we not ourselves known some of these quiet workers, whose influence lay in *being*, rather than in *doing*? Whose doings, at any rate (while they are among the eternal things which cannot die) were all in the natural and humble sphere in which God had placed them.

But when I say this, I do not mean that we should shut ourselves out from the great world around us, of which we form a necessary and integral part. There is an increasing tendency, especially in London, to isolation; and the best sort of people are often those who rather foster the tendency than fight against it. The man who lives next door is a stranger to us. And sometimes it seems necessary, in the interests of self-preservation, to continue this undesirable attitude. We live our own little life. We move in our own limited circle of interest and pleasure, and without stopping to question or consider, leave the outer world to pursue its own way, and take care of itself. Thus this great hive of human activity consists more and more of isolated cells, each separated from its neighbour. And the question of the text, "Where is Abel thy brother?" comes home to us with an added emphasis, amid the complex conditions of our modern life.

When we think of our own metropolis, this vast London, and of the problem of housing and employing its indigent poor, when we contemplate this beating heart of the great city, and think of the rival claims and multiform interests of society, we cannot but feel that it is a very strong temptation to encourage this isolation of which I have spoken.   And it is for the Church, as an institution, and for communicants, as individual members of that institution, to do what they can to break down this self-erected barrier between man and man.   Sympathy will go a long way. In any parish where the Church is strong and in-fluential, where she is in touch with her people, and kindly feeling exists between all classes, the evil of isolation is lessened, where it is not destroyed, and the question, " Where is Abel, thy brother ? " is not heard in the same accents of reproachful warning.

The Church is an institution admirably con-stituted to accomplish this end.   She appeals to the highest motives.   She works widely and yet indirectly by her prayers, her teaching, and her varied organizations, for the welfare of all.   It is her mission " to visit the fatherless and widows in their affliction," "and to see that such as are in need and necessity have right."   This is one side of Christian duty ; one half of the great

law of love. For human responsibility is of two
kinds, since all our obligations resolve themselves
into these two primary duties of love to God
and love to our neighbour.

These are nearly related, and they are suggested
to us by those two questions said to be addressed
by God Himself to man in the early days of
human history, the questions, "Where art thou?"
"Where is Abel thy brother?" These questions
read us searching lessons on our duty to ourselves,
our neighbour, and our God. They speak to
us as the children of one parent, who, above all
else, are dependent upon a father's love and care.

In answering these questions honestly and faithfully, we shall solve some of the problems of life,
and avoid some of its temptations. For they have
nothing to do with the mere accidents of life, but
with life itself, its essence, its inner relations, its
first duties. Only let us loyally and steadfastly
fulfil these in the strength of Christ our Master,
and we shall by no means lose our reward.

## IV.

## FEAST OF S. MATTHIAS.

## Faults of Good Men.

1 SAMUEL ii. 30.

"Them that honour Me I will honour, and they that despise Me
shall be lightly esteemed."

THE reason for the selection of 1 Samuel ii. 27,
as one of the Old Testament Lessons for
S. Matthias' Day, is to be found, without doubt,
in the concluding verse but one, "And I will
raise Me up a faithful priest, that shall do
according to that which is in Mine heart and in
My mind; and I will build him a sure house;
and he shall walk before Mine anointed for ever."
The teaching of the whole chapter, however,
is one of solemn warning, springing out of the
strong contrast presented between the rejected
and the promised priest; and as the Feast of
S. Matthias falls within the season of Lent,

it seems more appropriate to dwell upon the fact of Eli's defection, rather than upon the promise of a worthy successor, with which the Lesson ends.

The opening chapters of the First Book of Samuel are historically important from the clear and vivid pictures which they give of the rude times of the Judges, in the days before a settled monarchy, when the highest offices in Church and State were amalgamated in the person of a weak, almost blind and decrepit old man, whose lot it was to exercise priestly functions, and give judgment for the nation in secular causes.

In the very nature of things it was impossible that such a state of affairs could last. It was the "reductio ad absurdum" of both civil and religious government, when two such weighty and responsible offices as those of Chief Ruler and High Priest of Israel were committed to the feeble hands of an aged Levite, who, in the unrestrained licentiousness of his two wicked and profligate sons, Hophni and Phinehas, proved himself unequal to the task of governing even his own family and household.

In the person of Eli, we take leave of those earlier experiences of the chosen people, on their first settlement in Canaan, of which we

read in the Book of Judges, and pass at once,
with only the intervening years of Samuel's
rule, to the most ambitious and eventful period
of Jewish history, in which, under a more
consolidated form of government, the nation rose
rapidly to wealth and importance, during the
reigns of its three first and greatest kings—Saul
the strong, David the good, and Solomon the
wise.

The figure of Eli is familiar to us all,
as the kind patron of Samuel, the boy prophet,
who rose at length to be Israel's greatest Judge.
Eli's age and position, his mild and gentle rule,
are things associated with the earliest recollections
of our childhood ; and his name is endeared to
us, chiefly through its connection with the
noble youth who grew up under his roof and
training, and who was destined, eventually, to
act as his successor in the government and
administration of Jewish affairs.

The character of Eli, however, is one which
needs careful interpretation. His was one of
those mixed natures, which we often meet with
in the Bible, in which the good and the evil
are so blended, that it is difficult to say which
we admire or condemn most. There is no
question respecting Eli's motives. His piety
and good intentions were above suspicion. He

was possessed of a mind naturally religious and devout. His heart was innocent as that of a child. In his gentleness, amiability, and patient resignation, he was a pattern to all. He was singularly free, too, from feelings of a jealous or vindictive nature, for he had no ambitions ; yet, notwithstanding all this, Eli was essentially a weak man ; all his actions prove it. He lacked courage. He was sadly wanting in firmness and energy. Thus, he made a bad ruler, a weak parent, an inefficient priest. He was wholly unfitted to rule. His timid policy, his proneness to mistake, his utter inability to understand or influence others, were frequent causes of failure and disgrace.

When men of feeble will, like Eli, subscribe their names to any movement, the fact itself is generally enough to ensure its not succeeding.

We see him still, as he is represented in the early chapters of the First Book of Samuel, a not unfamiliar type of an easy-going good man, of heavy and ponderous build, living to a ripe old age, not a person of very keen sensibilities, his virtues all of the passive kind, representing only the milder side of religion, and even these clouded by habitual inertia, and a fatal tendency to procrastinate.

Such was Eli, a man guilty of no public crimes,

but only of private indiscretions and indolent omissions of duty, which yielded, however, in the end a full harvest of sorrows, not punished very severely, in his own person, but the cause of frightful woes which came afterwards upon his descendants and people.

A truly religious man at heart, feeling the loss of the Ark and the insult offered to the Divine Honour, more than the defeat of Israel and the death of his two sons. We should, I suppose, have called him "a conscientious man," in the sense that he satisfied himself. Those who do so generally find others who will take them at their own valuation, and believe that what they think and say of themselves is true. "A man who has never quarrelled with himself," is the definition which someone has given of such persons. And though Eli was no doubt a very favourable example of this stamp of man, yet we must concede, I think, that he belonged to that class of weak, conscientious persons which I have described, who, while doing a great deal of harm by their mistakes and omissions, yet never for a moment suspect that any blame lies at their own door, or is attached to their own ministry.

Think of the blind pertinacity with which he mistook the motive of Hannah, as she knelt in silent prayer, on the occasion of her first recorded visit to Shiloh ; or witness again, the tardy incapacity of his slow and halting mind, in the case of Samuel, where the Divine summons had to be repeated time after time, before it occurred to Eli that the Lord had called the child. How like the bewildered attempts of many an inefficient pastor who is for ever blundering in cases of conscience. The reproofs and advice of such people, even when given in the kindest spirit, and from the loftiest motives, somehow fail in their intention, and generally seem calculated to do mischief. Despite his undoubted piety and many good qualities, Eli was a man of this kind. His slow and tedious efforts to take in the circumstances of the case, led him to misjudge Hannah, and to withhold his advice from Samuel, for it was only by slow and painful steps that he acquired a correct view, and was enabled to act accordingly. Nevertheless, despite these obvious shortcomings, though he fell far below the level of a truly great man, yet we always think and speak of Eli as a good man, and such indeed he was. His faults were the faults of good men, his mistakes were their mistakes.

It is to well-intentioned and religious people, therefore, that the chief failings of Eli's life seem more especially to address themselves. He stands before us, no doubt, first of all, as a warning to feeble rulers and inefficient clergy. But it is not only in the Cabinet or the Church that his faults find imitators. His example speaks to other professions also. Whenever men are guilty of weak concessions and flagrant omissions of duty, they are followers of Eli.

In departments of life far removed from the vocation of a clergyman, we meet the same familiar figure in the feeble parent, the indifferent teacher, the indolent tradesman, who, though people may speak of him as a harmless, easy-going man, nevertheless, fails in everything that he undertakes, and blunders in all his relations with mankind. The dress may be changed, and the uniform discarded, but the man himself is in all essentials the same. He is the counterpart of Eli, a person who, notwithstanding his many excellent qualities, was yet the subject of some of the sharpest warnings ever uttered by heaven, and upon whose house there descended some of the deepest woes ever inflicted upon a single family.

Thus, while the human verdict generally passed upon Eli is on the whole flattering, the Divine verdict is simply scathing in its severity. As Israel's High Priest and a truly devout and religious man, it might naturally be supposed that Eli would be classed among those who honoured God in the highest sense of the term ; and yet it was to Eli that those solemn words were spoken, "Them that honour Me I will honour, and they that despise Me shall be lightly esteemed."

From which we learn that the Almighty is more honoured by a consistent example than by any combinations whatever of service and profession, except in so far as these are a faithful echo of our life.

If the death of Eli and his sons was the first tragic fulfilment of the Divine prophecy foretold concerning his house, it was no less a fitting representation of the fall of Jewish independence and of the ultimate extinction of the priesthood from the line of Ithamar. "Ichabod" was the name given to one of the successors to this falling house, the name given by his dying mother as she caught the evil tidings which fell from the lips of the messenger as he returned from the field of battle. "Ichabod," "the glory is departed."

Here, then, was a tragedy in three generations. And towards this terrible climax of pain and sorrow, of shame and defeat, many causes had been combining in the past.

The hour when the rotten tree falls is usually preceded by years of silent decay. Thus, the seeds of weakness and irresolution sown in the earlier days of Eli's rule were now bearing their bitter fruits. The reins of government had long been slipping from his feeble hands. There was no reserve of faith or patriotism stored up in the heart of the nation to offer effective resistance to a bold and determined foe. Religion had naturally declined and fled from a sanctuary where impious hands ministered only to profanity and crime.

The end had come. The sacred Ark, no longer the seat of mercy and the altar of national religion, had been dragged from its shrine at Shiloh, and placed at the head of the army. This was no pillar of fire to guide the people to victory or rest. Rather was it the pitiful invocation of an apostate Church for the intervention of one whom she had long denied. It spoke not of God, but of a fallen priesthood. It represented, not faith, but presumption; not the inspired confidence of a brave soldiery and an intrepid people, but only cowardice and superstition. It was a public confession of degradation.

And yet, like a single star shining out on a dark night, the one bright spot in this tragic story is the personal faith and piety of the venerable priest himself. Eli's own fortunes and those of his family, the defeat of the nation, the rout of the army, all these were secondary to this climax of woe, " The Ark of God was taken."

Thus, Shiloh was no more. Its sanctuary was deserted, the Jewish altar was profaned, and the sacred Ark itself was in the hands of heathen captors. It was this that struck the aged priest, and carried home his death-blow, "for his heart trembled for the Ark of God."

From the history of Eli, then, we glean two lessons. One is, that religion, where it does not influence character, cannot protect us either from the censure of man or the judgment of God. Another lesson is that sins of omission and passive neglect may be expected to bear active fruits of lawless insubordination, either in ourselves or our children. Out of those easy, self-indulgent vices, for which we find such ready excuse, will grow up in years to come strong passions, rank and strong, grievous sins, deriving their poison from the withered roots of many an incapacitated wish and many a weakened resolution. It may appear to us that there is no natural connection between the mild and passive faults of Eli's character and the wild licentiousness of his two godless sons. We find it difficult, in the weakness and self-indulgence of the father, to trace the parentage of those fierce, ungovernable passions, and that coarse brutality, which we discover in Hophni and Phinehas. But we know that sins, like plants or animals, change their character with their circumstances and surroundings. Self-indulgence in an old man often differs exceedingly from self-indulgence in a younger man. For example, anger in the former may show itself only in querulousness; in the latter it will burst forth in flaming passion, or a cruel and vindictive thirst for revenge. Thus, sins of omission and commission are nearly related, and passive faults of ease and self-indulgence prove, in the end, the parents of more scandalous crimes.

It was, perhaps, the one sentence which we should have least suspected in the case of so good a man as Eli that he should be classed among the despisers of the truth. And yet, it is a sentence which has been fulfilled over and over again in the history of weak-kneed professors, whose inconsistencies have set up a target for reproach, and whose lives, even more than their beliefs, have proved the rock of offence upon which others have stumbled.

Many a wide and lasting schism has arisen in this way. Such men are the authors of more heresies than even false and wayward teachers, and lead to graver scandals in the Church than do the vices of open and notorious sinners, because they give greater occasion to the enemies of the Lord to blaspheme.

Let us pray, then, to be saved, not only from sins of worldliness and unbelief, but also from sins of weakness and inconsistency, which

betray the trust imposed upon us, and open
again the pierced wounds of the Saviour's
bleeding side.

Do we not in the Litany ask to be delivered
from "blindness," as well as " hardness" of heart?
and from "hypocrisy," which is a sin of no less
danger than " contempt " of God's holy Word and
Commandment?   Only through the answer to
that prayer can we hope to be made "pillars in
the Temple of our God," or learn, in our own
experience, the better half of that true saying,
" Them that honour Me I will honour, and they
that despise Me shall be lightly esteemed."

The rejection of the House of Eli from the
Levitical priesthood carries a solemn warning to
all, and forms a not inappropriate teaching for the
season of Lent.   It acquires an added significance
when we remember that it is one of the selected
Lessons for the Feast of S. Matthias.   For, read
in the light of the Epistle for that festival, we are
led to regard it as the Old Testament counterpart
of the still more awful rejection which took place
in the expulsion of Judas from the number of the
twelve apostles.

S. Matthias did not add to their number.  He
was not chosen like S. Paul, or S. Barnabas, to
supply the growing needs of a rapidly expanding
Church; he only filled up the gap made in the

ranks of the apostles themselves. For he was
the actual substitute and successor in "the
ministry from which Judas by transgression fell."
And as such, he was selected by Divine lot,
contrary, it might seem (from the surname
already given to Barsabas), to the expectation,
perhaps even the wishes, of the Eleven. He was
the first of that holy band not personally called
and chosen by the Saviour Himself. Hence, his
appointment by Divine selection. In this he is a
type of the true pastor in all ages, whose hope
and confidence it is that he is the subject of a
Divine call.

Since the Feast of S. Matthias always falls
*about* (generally a little *before*) the Ember Season,
preceding the Lent Ordination, the petition in the
Collect, that "the Church may alway be preserved from false apostles, and may be ordered
and guided by faithful and true pastors," is
singularly appropriate. And the double lesson
contained in the rejection of Eli and Judas forms
an Ember teaching of no little weight and
solemnity.

It is a serious responsibility to occupy posts
vacated by men better and wiser than ourselves.
It is an even greater responsibility to stand where
others have fallen, to enter upon work in which
others have failed, or tread in the footprints of

E

those who, notwitstanding their gifts and opportunities, have somehow missed their way.

Such, however, was the position of Matthias, and in its wider aspect it is the position of all who bear the yoke of Christ, and take office in His Church and Kingdom. The thought is indeed a solemn one, and if it were not for the promised grace of God, it might well act as a deterrent to such as take Orders, and hope to serve in the ministry of the Gospel. To most of us, however, the tendency to forget, and to make light of warnings, is even greater than the tendency to exaggerate them. Hence it follows that the lessons suggested have a very proper place, and may well be included among other teachings for the Feast of S. Matthias.

## V.

## ASH WEDNESDAY.

### An Unavailing Repentance.

HEBREWS xii. 17.

"For he found no place of repentance, though he sought it
carefully with tears."

WITH regard to those whose biographies appear
in the earlier books of the Bible, it is
suggestive of very solemn reflections to note
how their history closes in the Old Testament
and how it opens again in the New Testament.
The contrast bids us be cautious how we judge of
individuals by what they appear at particular
times, or on particular occasions, showing how
differently He, Who reads the whole life, with
its context and conclusion, may judge from
what we ourselves do, who read but a part. For
example, Old Testament history leaves Esau
performing a pious and reverential act of mourn-

ing beside his father's grave, where, years after the touching reconciliation with Jacob at Penuel, the brothers again meet on friendly terms, and Esau agrees to bury for ever the memory of the wrongs once suffered at the hands of his younger brother. And yet, the death of Isaac was, above all other events, that most calculated to re-open the flood-gates of Esau's anger. Indeed, the old man's life was, at one time, Jacob's only safeguard, since it was the sole bond of union between the divided brothers; Esau's love for Isaac constituting the only reason for his forbearance towards Jacob. But now, summoned from their distant homes by their father's decease, the two brothers, the deceiver and the deceived, meet to mingle their tears in friendly competition, while each vies with the other in his eagerness to pay the last tribute of outward respect to the memory of their revered parent. Not a syllable occurs in the sacred narrative to indicate that the reconciliation between the two sons was other than perfect and complete. Nor does a single reproach escape from the lips of Esau, to mar the free forgiveness by which, once for all, he had cancelled the deep debt of revenge which he owed his treacherous and wily brother. So much for the generosity of Esau. Returning to his wild roving life in Edom, he appears to

have recognised that the covenant blessings and
promised land were to be his brother's, and,
with no little nobility of mind, to have acquiesced
in the Divine decision which had mapped out
for himself the lower place.   And yet, if we turn
to the pages of the New Testament, we are
startled to read in words of sad but scathing condemnation, this reference to the brave and generous
son of Isaac, "Lest there be any profane person
as Esau, who, for one morsel of meat sold his
birthright," . . . who "found no place of
repentance, though he sought it carefully with
tears."

We have, I suppose, all felt for Esau.   We
cannot but admire the high-spirited, sympathetic,
generous nature of the wild Edomite chief.
But we forget, in our admiration, the unrestrained
impulse, the uncurbed passion, the utter volatility
and instability of character which lay beneath
those more romantic traits which we have
described, faults so common in temperaments
like his.   How often, for example, do we find
the courage which will brave any danger, and
which is ready to carry its life in its hand
upon the hunting-ground or the battle-field,
associated with just that thoughtless inability
to estimate rightly the true value of things,
which we perceive in Esau, willing to barter

for insignificant trifles the greatest gifts of life, the products of the intellect, or the fortunes of the soul, for the gratification of a moment, selling the birthright of privilege for a mess of pottage.

There are noble exceptions to this rule ; yet, too often, those warm impulsive natures, which we all admire for their manly vigour and their honest hearts, are the first and easiest victims to the allurements of passion. Brilliant, witty, generous, courageous, they stake all, and they forfeit all, on the cast of a single die. Their impetuosity is their ruin, for lack of principle, of forethought, of steady persevering effort, of strong inflexible purpose, which holds on and refuses to give up, and says, " I will not let Thee go, except Thou bless me," such men sink to an early and dishonoured grave. En- dowed with uncommon gifts, and encouraged by the prospect of a splendid future, they nevertheless succumb to indolence, drink, or sensuality, while the light wind of passion carries them along like straws to their doom.

Over each of these slaves of impulse we may write the sad epitaph, " Thus Esau despised his birthright." That transaction with his brother, Jacob, gives us the key to his weak impetuous character, for simple as was the incident in itself, it speaks volumes respecting the nature and destiny of Esau the Elder. So graphically is the scene portrayed, so naturally and so completely does the man stand out before us, that if the actions of a lifetime had been preserved and handed down in the annals of a consecutive biography, we could scarcely have obtained a more thorough insight into the nature and feelings of the individual described, than is given us in the few verses to which we allude. So faithful is the picture, that it is difficult to persuade ourselves that we were not eye-witnesses of the scene. There, busy in the tent, is the cautious, wily Jacob, always ready to perceive and make the most of an advantage; and, just entering it, is his more simple, manly, but impetuous, brother returning weary and disappointed from a long day's unsuccessful hunting, faint and desperate, smelling the savoury broth which Jacob had prepared, and counting the present worth of a little food more than the value of a hundred birthrights.

The original words of the text inimitably convey to us the eager greed with which, in a half-finished sentence, he utters his passionate desire, " Feed me with some of that red," while with the depth and cunning of the arch-tempter himself his brother at once sees his

opportunity, and presses his advantage in the
words, "Sell me this day thy birthright," and
Esau said, "I am going to die, and what profit
shall this birthright do to me?" "And Jacob
said, Swear to me this day; and he swear
unto him; and he sold his birthright unto
Jacob," "And he did eat and drink, and rose
up, and went his way: Thus Esau despised his
birthright."

Such is the oft-told tale of eager passion
and unrestrained impulse, of a desire which
will take no denial, and brook no delay, which
cannot pause to think or wait to consider,
which ignores the future, regardless of
consequences, and sees only the present, and
in the exaggerated reality of an immediate
gratification is ready to forfeit innocence, opportunity, and peace of mind, the best things of
this life, and the better things of that which
is to come, for a little food, or a little drink,
for a day's pleasure, or an evening's debauch.
And this is profanity—that "profane person,"
Esau. The word means "forth-from" (without)
a temple. It describes the man whose aspirations
are limited to this life only, who is sense-
bound, who values everything from a worldly
standpoint. The man who passing-forth and
leaving the circle of all spiritual influences has

no temple in the heart, and no temple in nature, to whom nothing testifies of God, "being alienated from the life of God, through the ignorance that is in him."

And such is every slave of impulse, a "profane person," as was Esau.

I do not, of course, wish to be understood as speaking dogmatically upon the subject of Esau's repentance. Whether or not he ultimately found mercy with God is not the question here raised by Scripture. The repentance spoken of in the Epistle to the Hebrews is that in which he pleads with his blind father Isaac for the forfeited blessing. A blessing which in truth he had lost years before, when, in a thoughtless moment, he parted with his birth-right. And so far as it concerned his birthright, this repentance with all its bitter anguish was fruitless, and unavailing, since, in that respect, "there was found no place of repentance, though he sought it carefully with tears."

And so Esau's unavailing sorrow is taken as an abiding picture of those tears of remorse which do not wipe away sin, but which are shed only to be shed over again. Thus, while Scripture is silent respecting Esau's hereafter, yet the loss of his birthright, together with the covenant privileges and prophetic blessing, do leave in the mind a sad unanswered doubt, even with regard to the long hereafter, concerning the rejector of those privileges.

But when speaking of Esau, I wish to be understood as discussing a case of life-failure, and not as pronouncing finally upon his acceptance or rejection in the world to come. Of such life-failures as are recorded in Holy Scripture perhaps the two for which the heart bleeds most, are those exhibited in the persons of Esau and Absalom. No doubt there are others but none, I think, which so strongly enlist our sympathies as the unfortunate son of David, and the scarcely less unfortunate son of Isaac. For Judas, we have no tears. Saul, we can but half pity. Even Reuben's downfall provokes but little feeling on his behalf, because so few particulars of his life are given. But with Esau and Absalom it is otherwise. The beauty of the one, and the manliness of the other, are still before us. The tears and laments of David over his rebellious but much loved son have been repeated by thousands, while the trembling agitation of the blind, decrepit old man, the patriarch Isaac, and the impassioned prayers and tears of his erring first-born, so heart-felt and so unavailing, have touched some of the deepest and tenderest chords which the

human heart can sound.   And as we read
to-day of that unavailing repentance, let us
gather from it a timely warning for ourselves;
while we learn that it is not in sorrow, and not
in tears alone, that peace and forgiveness are won,
but in the steadfast resolve which turns from
its evil ways, and in the faith which lays hold
on the proffered grace of God : as it is written,
not he which confesseth, but he which " confesseth
and forsaketh his sins shall have mercy."

# VI.

## FIRST SUNDAY IN LENT.

### A Worldly Choice.

GENESIS xiii. 10-13.

"And Lot lifted up his eyes, and beheld all the plain of Jordan, that it was well watered every where, before the Lord destroyed Sodom and Gomorrah, even as the garden of the Lord, like the land of Egypt, as thou comest unto Zoar. Then Lot chose him all the plain of Jordan; and Lot journeyed east: . . . and Lot dwelled in the cities of the plain, and pitched his tent toward Sodom. But the men of Sodom were wicked and sinners before the Lord exceedingly."

LOT is one of the mixed characters of the Bible, not like Abraham, Moses, or Daniel; nor again like Cain, Absalom, or Judas. He is not a person you can admire or point to as a hero; neither can you heap upon him unqualified condemnation

There are some men so much better than ordinary people, they stand on such a high platform, their life is so much above our own, that we are accustomed to think of them as altogether good, though they are not so.

Lot's family (even those who had escaped its destruction) and reproduced itself in their own and their father's shame.

We naturally regard those who sacrifice their children's faith and virtue to worldly and ambitious motives as partaking of the sin of Lot, yet how common it is for parents to be indifferent to the religious welfare of their offspring. For the sake of some trifling worldly advantage they will expose them to really serious temptations. The same parents who would refuse a good appointment for their sons in an unhealthy district in a tropical climate, would eagerly accept such an appointment in a firm of questionable character, or would freely embark them in a business where the almost certain price of their advancement would be moral ruin.

But in estimating the character of Lot, while admitting his flagrant worldliness, we must, on the other hand, remember what strength of purpose, and what a depth of conviction was needed to enable a man during a long residence in Sodom to retain his integrity, and even to acquire a useful and dominant influence in the place. It was, no doubt, culpably weak of Lot to go there, and no less culpably worldly for him to remain there, but it was, nevertheless, a proof of uncommon strength of mind that he could play so dangerous a part, and yet adhere to his profession and faith, amid influences so deadly and seductive.

Some men's spiritual surroundings are all helpful. They have the advantage of a careful training and a pious home. They have none of the trials and temptations which others encounter. It was so at first with Lot. During his early days he was helped, not hindered, taken by the hand, guided wisely, and so led to do greater and nobler things than he would either have attempted or accomplished by himself. Thus, he appeared a stronger and better man than he really was. The cup of trial was not yet placed in his hand. His hour of temptation had not yet come. For one thing, Lot was Abraham's nephew. That in itself was no trifling advantage. Again, Abraham, we read, "Took Lot his brother's son" with him, when he set out for Palestine. Thus he began to be identified with his uncle. Already they had left Haran and its heathen associations behind them. So far, Lot was advancing. He had joined his fortunes with those of the father of the faithful, and all went well. His prospects improved. His future brightened. His substance increased. He grew wealthy. But at this point a change comes over the character of Lot. Abraham could stand the test of riches. Lot could not. Prosperity did not spoil the steadfast mind of Abraham ; it betrayed the worldly heart of Lot. Previous to this he was more or less identified with his uncle. The goodness of the one cast a veil over the weakness of the other. While Abraham planned and carried out what was done, in all things noble, Lot was merely passive. For example, it was Abraham that heard the call of God, Abraham that made the momentous decision, and calling his household together, made all arrangements for his departure in obedience to that call. Abraham that bid farewell to his home and kindred, and set forth, as the world's pioneer, the first pilgrim, the first emigrant in that westward march, which has been going on ever since. It was the first step in the progress of the race. In all this Lot was passive. He only accompanied Abraham. Then, on the journey, each pause was marked by its own special act of worship and thanksgiving. Each temporary settlement of these early colonists was consecrated by an altar being reared to the honour of God, and for the purpose of divine worship. The movements of Abraham might have been traced by the rude churches which he left behind him as mementoes of his progress and safe transport. Abraham could not reside in a place where he had no centre of worship, and no means of communion with God. But Lot is never once mentioned in this connection. It was Abraham that built these altars, and Abraham that called upon the name of the Lord. For like so many whose surroundings are religious, Lot had but a feeble interest in these things.

Thus, in all that is recorded, until his separation from Abraham, Lot played a merely secondary and subordinate part. The vision was not his, the decision was not his, the thanksgiving was not his. For a while, and to his own benefit, he followed the stronger will of his uncle, but at the point where he grew rich, he began to act with independence. He threw off the leadership of Abraham, and commenced to act for himself. Immediately we discover his true nature. It was the turning-point of Lot's career. From that moment he went wrong. Each step is downwards, each decision brings with it loss and degradation. For as water always seeks to find its level (though temporarily banked up) so in those whose religious surroundings, and careful home training, are above their tastes and natural dispositions, there is a constant tendency (when these restraints are withdrawn) to sink to their real level of thought and conduct and profession.

The chief points then in the history of Lot are indicated for us in the following brief records :—

"Abraham took Lot," and "Lot went with him."

At this time, Lot's star was in the ascendant, and had he continued to follow the good influences which are indicated in these words, he might have become a truly great man. He was under the guidance of Abraham, and was willing to follow his leadership and example. He had left Ur of the Chaldees, and, joining his fortunes with those of the heir of all the promises (braving danger and difficulty), had set forth and reached with Abraham the land of promise. And then it follows :—

"And Lot also . . . had flocks, and herds, and tents." Lot grew rich, and his wealth became a source of temptation to him. "And Lot lifted up his eyes, and beheld all the plain of Jordan, that it was well watered everywhere." Here came the turning-point of his life, the temptation which exposed his worldly heart, and betrayed him into taking the first false step. Still Lot might have retreated and withdrawn from Sodom, but the unhappy choice, once made, proved lasting in its consequences ; for "Lot journeyed east," going backwards from the course on which he and Abraham had set forth. "And Lot dwelled in the cities of the plain, and pitched his tent toward Sodom." The inclination once yielded to quickly hurries us into still further dangers. "And Lot sat in the gate of Sodom," probably holding some civil office and authority as judge or magistrate; for even in Sodom integrity had weight; and the stranger who came only to sojourn remained to be a factor in its social life and public affairs. Thus, Lot became more and more identified with Sodom, and every day he lived there it became less possible to leave it; until by a miracle of mercy (and in answer to Abraham's intercessions) he was delivered from the ruin in which he was involved.

"The people of Sodom perished in their own corruption," but the one righteous man who dwelt there in culpable indifference to the perils to which he exposed himself and his children is commemorated still in the local name given to the Dead Sea—'Bahr Lut,' the Sea of Lot." * Surely it is a sad commemoration, for while it marks out Lot as the only person worthy of distinction, in connection with the cities of the plain, yet it does so in a way that adds significance to his fall, and to the fact that his family shared in the judgment which descended upon the inhabitants of Sodom and Gomorrah.

I have spoken of Lot as one of the mixed characters of Old Testament history. One reason

* Dean Farrar.

why the Bible so often gives us these mixed
characters is that they are life portraits. They
are not fictitious persons, creatures of the imagination. They are real characters whom we see as
they really were. But another reason is that such
persons, in their weaknesses and faults, often carry
important lessons for others. For we can hardly
fail to see in them likenesses to ourselves.

When we read of a notoriously wicked person,
we unconsciously assume that the wicked things
he did, carry no lesson to us, because we feel no
temptation to such hideous faults as he was guilty
of. " I could never be like that," we say; "this
man is a monster of iniquity, and is repulsive to
me in the extreme."

Again, the very good people seem too much
above us to stimulate active endeavour. We
think that we can never attain to such excellence
as they possess.

But the man of mixed motives and inferior
attainments, the man who has some nobility and
many good points, but who, nevertheless, is of
like passions with ourselves, appeals at once to
our needs and desires. His faults are our faults.
His better nature, too, is what we find something
of in ourselves. We long to imitate his success ;
we tremble lest we should copy his mistakes.
Altogether (being on our own level) his good and

bad points, alike, read us home lessons which we can feel and understand. And that is why the Bible portrays so many mixed characters of the ordinary type.

Now in Lot we have a man of this stamp. He was a good man in many respects; and had he used the best influences in his life, and cultivated the helps which Providence sent him, he might have been a still stronger man. But when he separated from Abraham, he lost the anchor which bound him to what was highest and noblest. Think what it must have meant to substitute the companionship of Abraham and his kinsfolk for the influences of Sodom. Yet this was the sacrifice which he made in order to satisfy his worldly desires. In other words, he sacrificed honour and peace of mind, he lost his coveted possessions, he lost his wife, and some of his children, and had the pain and grief of seeing the remnant grow up in self-indulgence and sin; and all this hinged upon that one deliberate act of worldly choice, which led him to take the slippery and dangerous path. You can scarcely call it an act of wilful sin. It was like choosing a questionable business because of its profitableness. It was trying to serve God and mammon.

The two points which I would emphasize are, that Lot had capabilities of goodness which he let slip, helps which he rejected from worldly motives. He had no vices. He did not cast off his faith. He appears to have retained his integrity. But he lived near to the world, sought it for its profit, and suffered in consequence. The other lesson (and it is a very solemn one) is that a man's self is not revealed until temptation trys it. Lot was a follower of Abraham, but he had not the heart of Abraham. The question is, to which side does the bias of the mind turn? Is it towards good or towards evil? For a while all may go well, and men will see no difference in the characters of Abraham and Lot; but one day circumstances will combine to try our real nature, and the hidden self will assert itself. The saintly mind or the worldly heart will be revealed. Lot will separate from Abraham, and that separation will often prove the hinge and turning-point of the whole life.

My brothers! let us search ourselves, our motives, as well as our conduct; that we may know which way the prevailing bias leans. And let us pray that, in the hour of trial, when the strain comes, we may not be found wanting.

# VII.

## SECOND SUNDAY IN LENT.

### 𝕿𝖍𝖊 𝕻𝖗𝖊𝖘𝖊𝖓𝖈𝖊 𝖔𝖋 𝕲𝖔𝖉.

GENESIS xxviii. 16.
" Surely the Lord is in this place; and I knew it not."

THESE words were not spoken in a church. They
were spoken on a wild moor, under the blue starlit
sky of an eastern night, by a solitary traveller, at
the close of the day's wanderings, who, weary and
benighted, had lain him down to sleep, with only
the rough stones for his pillow. And as he slept
he dreamed, and his dream was so remarkable
and its effect upon his mind so impressive and
salutary, that it proved a real and undoubted crisis
in the dreamer's life. And the first words he
uttered on waking were the words of the text,
" Surely the Lord is in this place; and I knew it
not." It is needless for me to say that the
traveller was the patriarch Jacob, and the dream
the vision of Bethel.

To Jacob that sleep was a real awaking; it was like the acquisition of a new sense. It was a conscious appropriation by the mind of a truth which at once woke up the slumbering soul, with all the better instincts of the man's nature, and drew forth the latent strength of his character, giving a new and definite impulse to his whole life. Yet it was communicated during physical sleep.

It formed an entirely new experience to the patriarch. In that dream he had made a conscious discovery. During that night spent in the lonely desert, he had learned what more than seventy years of active life had failed to teach him. You may call it imagination, fancy, an impression, merely; but call it what you will, it was to Jacob a real and abiding influence, a lifelong possession, an acquisition which he never lost. It was the conscious finding of what so many are seeking, a gift for which the soul pines, without which it cannot rest or be satisfied, and that gift is a revelation of *Deity*. To Jacob it came as a sense of the presence of God. And this leads me to remark that it is possible for us to know much and yet remain ignorant of God. For example, a man may receive a good education, he may be well-read, and mix with thoughtful and intelligent people. He may know the world, and lead a busy and active life. His brain may be stored with information on a variety of subjects. And yet he may lack that which Jacob, when an old man of nearly eighty, found so suddenly and unexpectedly. For it is undeniable that there are truths apprehended by the mind and appropriated by the soul which cannot be communicated in the ordinary way by means of the senses. It is so with all spiritual acquisitions. They are appropriated by faith. You can offer no positive and direct proof of their existence. Take this realisation of God's presence to a devout soul. It is not a something you can touch. It is not a something you can see. None of the senses bear witness to that presence. And yet, if you possess it, it may be to you a fact as real and unquestioned as the consciousness of your own being. And like Jacob you may awake from the sleep of years, or the dream of a lifetime, to say, " Surely the Lord is in this place ; and I knew it not."

But let us look at the subject a little more in detail. The simplest form which the realisation of God's presence usually takes in the mind is that expressed by Hagar, when the angel met her by the well of water, in the Wilderness of Shur, as she fled from her mistress Sarai, and half in fear and half in joy she called the name of the Lord that spake unto her, " Thou God seest me."

To a devout mind the presence of God will become
much more than these words of Hagar express ;
but at first it is just that, " Thou God seest me."
An observing presence, an eye felt to be always
upon us, a look which reads us through and
through, the scrutiny of One to whom "all hearts
are open " and " all desires known."    The experience of Nathaniel, when Jesus said to him,
" Before that Philip called thee, when thou wast
under the fig-tree, I saw thee."    The experience
of the woman of Samaria, when in one sentence
Christ unveiled the secret of her unhappy life.
The experience of S. Peter, after his denial, when
the cock crew the second time, and " the Lord
turned, and looked upon Peter."    The experience
of Saul of Tarsus, when the risen Saviour, speaking from heaven, told him, what in his inner consciousness he knew full well, " It is hard for thee
to kick against the goad."    Any one of these
could (at the moment) have echoed these words
of the hundred and thirty-ninth Psalm, " O Lord,
Thou hast searched me, and known me.    Thou
knowest my down-sitting and mine uprising, Thou
understandest my thought afar off.    Thou com-
passest my path and my lying down, and art
acquainted with all my ways. . . . . Thou hast
beset me behind and before, and laid Thine hand
upon me. . . . . Whither shall I go from Thy

Spirit? or whither shall I flee from Thy presence?
If I ascend up into heaven, Thou art there; if I
make my bed in hell, behold, Thou art there. If
I take the wings of the morning, and dwell in
the uttermost parts of the sea; even there shall
Thy hand lead me, and Thy right hand shall hold
me." Such is the presence of God to the newly
awakened soul. Such it was to Jacob. He had
fancied himself alone (miserably alone), and he
was startled to find that he was not alone, that
God was with him, even in the desert. And the
immediate effect of his discovery was fear. "He
was afraid, and said, How dreadful is this place!
this is none other but the house of God, and this
is the gate of heaven." And yet the vision of
Bethel was preeminently a vision of love. The
ladder reaching from earth to heaven, the
angels ascending and descending upon it, the
very stones of the wilderness forming a means
of communication with the skies, here was nothing
to alarm or terrify. It was the very gentlest mode
possible of dispelling the thought of his isolation
from God, of bridging over the seeming distance
between man and his Maker, teaching in one
lesson that God was both near and kind, and
that communion with Him was possible. Nay!
there was positive comfort and encouragement
in the lesson taught him; just such comfort and

encouragement as Jacob needed, for he was at that time lonely in more senses than one. The loneliness of the eastern desert was nothing to the loneliness of a blighted life and a desolate heart. Flying from the just anger of an injured brother, estranged from his relatives, unhappy in himself, thrust out from home and all the associations of his youth (now that he was no longer young), to begin life afresh and seek his fortunes elsewhere. And all this as the direct consequence of his own sin. One might suppose that the vision of Bethel would have been at once the very joy and rejoicing of his heart, and ultimately it became so, but at first he was afraid.

Thus we learn that the thought of God and the thought of sin when they enter the mind together produce fear. But we must be careful not to limit this sense of the presence of God to that awe-inspiring dread felt by Jacob, as he awoke from his memorable dream. The feeling is capable of a far nobler expression. For example, we may think of it as a restraining influence from sin, as a constraining influence towards duty, and as a consolatory influence under trial.

Take the case of Joseph. Was it not the secret of Joseph's constancy? Everything seemed combined to try his integrity to the utmost

on the occasion of his great temptation.   We
remember that Joseph was a slave in Potiphar's
house, with no home influences to restrain him,
no parents' grief or anger to deter him from
evil.   Years had passed away since he had
even heard the sacred name of the Hebrews'
God.   Probably, when he last heard it, in the
far distant land of his nativity, it was from
the lips of his aged father himself.   Joseph
was a mere youth when sold into Egypt, so
that his religious impressions could scarcely have
ripened into belief, and already he had sojourned
many years in that heathen land.   Then too,
he was just at an age, and just in that position,
which made the temptation most trying.   A
slave, with no family connections, unknown and
uncared for, yet enjoying a measure of prosperity
and indulgence such as might well have fostered
the very basest passions of his nature.   "All
these things were against him."   Like our
Blessed Lord Himself, he entered into his
temptation alone.   But as if the absence of any
human presence to aid him in the trial only
cast Joseph back upon his early belief in the
Divine Presence, in fear and anguish of soul,
he fled from contamination, crying, "How then
can I do this great wickedness, and sin against
God?"   That thought saved him "and sin

against God." It is the only safeguard in temptation.

Again, this sense of the presence of God is a source of strength, and will become a constraining influence towards duty. Take the case of Elijah. Was it not the secret of Elijah's confidence when he slew the idolatrous prophets at Carmel, and confronted Ahab, in the vineyard of Naboth the Jezreelite? His faith and courage were grounded upon an abiding sense of the presence of God. "As the Lord of Hosts liveth, before whom I stand," was the invariable introduction to his greatest acts. Elijah felt that he was not alone in his protests, that he acted all along as the inspired witness of Jehovah, in Whose presence he stood and served. Even in that darkest hour of his life, when he lay down under the juniper-tree, and wished for himself that he might die (he who never was to die), like S. Peter, sinking beneath the waves on the Lake of Galilee, he could not but fly to Him, in Whom, for the moment, he had failed to trust. Like a man suffering from asthma, and gasping for breath, struggling to rise and get more air, it was the instinct of life to Elijah to seek again that comfortable presence which, for a brief spell, he had forfeited, under the sense of isolation and failure. Such appears to be the

explanation of the prophet's flight to Horeb.
Nothing would satisfy him but to climb the
lofty peaks of Sinai, and stand where Moses
stood before him, and there (in the stillness
of the desert, where no human presence could
come between his soul and the Divine Presence)
lose in the loneliness of nature's solitudes the
loneliness of a saddened heart. Elijah's flight
to Horeb was the literal interpretation of so
many of David's psalms. It was the Dove
flying back to the Ark. The desire expressed
so forcibly in that devout modern hymn,
"Nearer, my God, to Thee, nearer to Thee ;
e'en though it be a cross that raiseth me."

Once more. The realisation of God's presence
is a consolatory influence in times of trial.
Take a New Testament example. It is no
longer the angel standing by Hagar's well,
nor the whirlwind, and fire, and tempest, sweeping
across the heights of Horeb ; it is not Joseph's
safeguard nor Jonah's fear ; it is the Saviour,
on the night of His Passion, with the beloved
disciple leaning on His breast, at the Last
Supper. That was the presence of God to
S. John.

My brothers! know you ought of this more
definite, this later form of that Presence of the
Man, and the Friend, and the Saviour, Christ ?

" God, Who at sundry times and in divers manners," revealed Himself unto our fathers in the days of old, by angels, by prophecy, by miracles, by dreams, by type and symbol, by the Tables of the Law in the hand of Moses, and the Urim and Thrummin on the breastplate of Aaron, by the fire and cloud which guided, and the manna which fed, His people, "hath in these last days spoken unto us by His Son."

All that went before was but as the shadow to the substance, compared with the gifts of Christian times.

Have we realised that thought?   Have we claimed our spiritual heritage?

My brothers! the presence of Christ is not a mere poetic fiction. It is a religious fact of almost universal experience. One of the latest promises of our Saviour to the individual believer, was, "If a man love Me, he will keep My words; and My Father will love him, and We will come unto him, and make Our abode with him." Again, we have that saying, "Where two or three are gathered together in My Name, there am I in the midst of them." What is this but the presence of Christ in public worship?

S. Luke's definition of an open Bible is, Jesus expounding "in all the scriptures the things

F

concerning Himself." What is this but the presence of Christ in Holy Scripture?

And whatever construction we may put upon those words, "This is My Body," all schools of interpretation agree that, to the believing soul, they suggest a blessed and spiritual presence of Christ in Holy Communion.

One word of appeal. Have you realised the presence of God as a restraining influence from sin? "Thou God seest me": as a constraining influence towards duty? "The love of Christ constraineth us": as a consolatory influence under trial? "The peace of God keeping the heart." Have you in your own persons experienced the presence of Christ, in the means of grace, as we call them? Do you meet God in the study of His Word? Do you commune with Him in prayer? Have you drawn from Christ real gifts in Holy Communion? Then you have learnt the Christian counterpart of Jacob's experience, when, in loneliness and guilt, he awoke from his memorable dream, and said, "Surely the Lord is in this place; and I knew it not."

# VIII.

## THIRD SUNDAY IN LENT.

### A Fruitful Life.

GENESIS xxxix. 23.

"The Lord was with Joseph, and that which he did, the Lord made it to prosper."

JOSEPH'S was a life hidden with God; sheltered by the Divine Presence. We always feel that the nestling wings were about him, and that he was the especial subject of God's protecting care and love. Yet he lived an active life; indeed he was the first of the patriarchs who did so. We think of him as the "Whittington" of those early days, the motherless boy who, from no wish of his own, was forced to leave home for the metropolis of ancient Egypt, the great emporium of trade and learning, "to make," as we should say, "his fortune."

Now, the simple lesson of the text, indeed the

lesson which lies upon the surface of the whole narrative, is, that God was with him all through that fruitful life.

Some men begin well and end sadly. It was so with Solomon. Their career opens in sunshine and closes in shadow. " A young saint, and old sinner," is a proverb which embodies this half-truth, which we thank God is not a universal truth. It is, however, a sad prophecy which has its own bitter fulfilment in the history of every Church, and the experience of every church-worker. The Garden of the Lord is no exception in this respect. Religion has bright blossoms that fall ere they set in fruit. We can all point to men who began well, and afterwards went astray. On the other hand, there are some who only give the dregs of their life to God. But Joseph did the happy thing. He gave the whole of it. For God was with him in his home, and in his exile : with him in his early dreams, and in the pit : with him in Potiphar's house, in the Egyptian dungeon, and in the chariot of Pharaoh's first officer of state. Three times it is noticed, in this same chapter from which the text is taken, that God "was with him " in prosperity, in adversity, in his life's work.

The first thing I wish you to observe about Joseph is, that while he lived near to God he was

separated from his brethren. Now, we may be
separated from our connections in a bad sense,
or, like Joseph, in a good sense, because the world
fails to comprehend our interests and motives·
We know that Joseph's was in a good sense,
because this trial in his home-life forms one out
of two points of resemblance between the patriarch
and our Saviour Christ. For He Who was holy,
harmless, and "separate from sinners," is pro-
phetically referred to as the medium of blessing
to others under this very figure. But we need
great caution in pointing to Joseph as an example,
in this early estrangement from his family. In
most cases, to be alienated from our near
relatives indicates some fault on our own part
rather than on theirs. It is not the grace of
Joseph, but the waywardness of Ishmael, that is
the cause. Some contradictory element in our
nature, a thorny temper, a jealous disposition, a
sharp tongue. It may arise from some constitu-
tional weakness which is allowed to detract from
the beauty of our character, and though, in this
case, we are only partly to blame, yet we should
be slow to judge others for their coolness or
aversion towards us. No one, however, feels more
acutely than a child what it is to be slighted and
misunderstood. And it is surely written for our
consolation at such times, that Joseph, through his

father's fondness and his own nobility, was despised and hated of his brethren.

We are accustomed, perhaps, to think of Joseph as the typical business man, shrewd and calculating, like his father, Jacob. A person of varied gifts and quick perceptions, able to adapt himself readily to circumstances. Some people lack this power altogether. They never change. You cannot transplant them. They are like those plants which thrive only on the soil on which they were raised. But though Jacob had the business acumen of his father Joseph, he inherited also something of the contemplative nature of his grandfather Isaac. It is a rare combination, seldom found except in truly great men. For example, there are plenty of clever students, and some thoughtful philosophers, but they are, for the most part, visionary in their aims, and unpractical in their endeavours. Such men are out of touch with everyday life. They have little in common with the prevailing thought and interests of mankind. It was otherwise with Joseph. Though a dreamer and a theorist, he possessed much practical common-sense ; and he united with these qualifications the enthusiasm of a great reformer, the energy of a great statesman, and the skill of a great financier. Joseph's life was interspersed with long periods of solitude ;

but these only served to prepare him for further activities.

First, there was the isolation of his youth, caused by the estrangement of his brothers. Cut off from all companions, he naturally sought interests and pursuits compatible with his loneliness. He cultivated a habit of meditation. He wandered in the fields, and when he spoke to any he related to them his thoughts. "Behold, this dreamer cometh," was the taunt with which his kinsmen greeted him. Even in those days Joseph was no mere herdsman. His mind was too full of great and noble aspirations for the mundane life which his brothers led. The waving cornfields in which he laboured (piling up the golden sheaves) created visions of wealth and greatness, which bore rich fruit afterwards in the heart of the philanthropic statesman. The stars, which had so often taught the Eastern astrologer in his midnight watch, had their silent lessons for the meditative youth. Joseph had need, afterwards, of all the lofty sentiments and bright visions of his boyhood to keep him pure and good. The love lavished upon him by his aged father was not lost on the motherless lad in the long dreary exile which followed his captivity in Egypt. His father's faith, and his father's affection were the two bonds which endeared him to his native land

and which kept him, in years to come, from the fetters of Egyptian superstition and the toils of Eastern licentiousness.

Again, there was the isolation of his long captivity. Surely, it was no light matter to be incarcerated for thirteen years in an Egyptian prison, under the stigma of an unjust sentence and a false charge. Joseph, however, left prison as he entered it, a pure, noble, fearless man. Such heroism is remarkable. It was not the result of his innocence merely, it was not that alone which buoyed up his drooping spirits through those sad, weary years. I have myself known an innocent man restored to liberty after a long period of false imprisonment, and the result was pitiable in the extreme. He returned to his friends, prematurely old, dwarfed alike in body and mind, crushed by years of hopeless captivity, and the severity of a prison life. When he regained his freedom you could scarcely regard him as a man ; the chain was still on his spirit ; the iron had entered into his soul. He resembled a maltreated animal ; he acted like a timid child. It was otherwise with Joseph. His lengthened captivity had done nothing to depress his ardent nature, or daunt his latent courage. He had lost nothing of his natural energy. He had rather acquired force, wisdom, dignity, by his long sequestration from the world. His mind had stored up glowing visions of the past and high hopes of the future. He was ready, at once, to step from the dungeon to the throne, from the warder's cell to the courtier's chair. His loneliness had only taught him independence, self-reliance, fortitude.

Now, weak minds are depressed by solitude, but great minds are often strengthened and elevated by it. We know that the passionate earnestness of S. John the Baptist had its root in solitude, and that the three pregnant years of Our Saviour's ministry were but the ripe ears which grew out of the thirty years of quiet seclusion which preceded them.

But I notice another thing. Joseph's piety was not unobserved. His master saw it. For even the world is not ignorant of the worth of true religion. Integrity has a commercial value, which the most irreligious taskmaster is not slow to appreciate.

Thus, we may take comfort from the fact that, if religion sometimes leads us to be scorned and hated, it also leads us to be honoured and feared. My brothers! it is a text for clerks, and business men; for all, indeed, who occupy positions of trust. "And his master saw that the Lord was with him, and that the Lord made all that he did to prosper in his hand, and Joseph found grace in his sight, and he served him ; and he made him overseer over his house, and all that he had he put into his hand."

Is it true, then, that religion is the surest road to success ? Surely it is so, if by success we mean that which is real and enduring. For the elevation of some people is like that of a balloon. It is but the travesty of greatness, the inflation of wealth, the ostentation of pride. There is nothing noble, nothing inspiring, about such an elevation. It is a mere nine days' wonder ; a thing to be looked at. It fulfils no object, and teaches no lesson. It is all show, ending in disaster and disgrace. The balloon is sure to fall, and it will generally come down faster than it went up. It is so with all fictitious greatness. The auspicious rise is succeeded by a most undignified descent, and the sudden inflation by a speedy collapse.

But Joseph's greatness was not of this kind. His life was great in the loftiness of its ideals, the simplicity of its motives, the wealth of its experience, and the richness of its reward.

What a varied and changeful life it was ! First a favourite son (always a dangerous honour), then a hated brother, next a helpless slave, then a trusted servant, then again a hopeless captive, and lastly a powerful ruler, with a great and lasting success. Truly it was an up and down life, and chequered with much trial and sorrow, yet one of infinite variety and extended usefulness. The links which bound together each separate act, and formed out of this changeful panorama a beauteous and consistent whole, were a childlike faith, a holy walk, a steadfast purpose, a lofty aim.

There is one lesson which, above all others, we glean from the life of Joseph. It is that a public life, a busy life, need not shut us out from the presence of God. For Joseph lived such a life, and yet was nearer to God than any of his brethren. For stirring scenes and crowding thoughts cannot, of themselves, separate us from Him, any more than the quiet and seclusion of a pastoral life can insure His nearness and love. And yet, to be the keeper of Potiphar's slaves, the warder of Pharaoh's state dungeon, the favoured courtier and commissioned Viceroy of Egypt, the honoured son-in-law of Potipherah, the Great High Priest of On, was a trying career for any man. Experiences such as these formed slippery steps for an unsophisticated youth to climb.

To change his name, but not his nature, to be allied with the very head of a corrupt heathen priesthood, and yet retain his Hebrew faith, to come fresh from the vines and cornfields of Palestine to mingle in the complex life of a great city, so as to be identified with it, in other words, to rule over Egypt, and be an Egyptian (in all but heart), was a triumph of greatness, a triumph of faith. And the secret of it all lay concealed in those few simple words, "The Lord was with Joseph, and that which he did, the Lord made it to prosper."

# IX.

## FOURTH SUNDAY IN LENT.

### Pessimism and Faith.

Genesis xlii. 36.

"All these things are against me."

Acts xx. 24.

"None of these things move me."

How like this is to the different way in which people still take their troubles, and face the trials and difficulties of life! Jacob and S. Paul were each speaking of their circumstances.

Jacob's was a mind full of timorous foreboding. He was what we should call a pessimist. He always expected the worst to happen, anticipating evils which never came. "Joseph is not," he cried, "and Simeon is not, and ye will take Benjamin away: all these things are against me."

Viewing life naturally, and apart from the promises of God, it seemed as if mountains of trial and difficulty confronted him.  The outlook was so dark that his whole life appeared overcast. And yet S. Paul was in reality exposed to far greater trials than Jacob.  But he viewed them from the Christian standpoint.  He saw the controlling hand of God in every event.  Under the most trying circumstances (though he knew that bonds and afflictions awaited him) he could still say, "None of these things move me."

This was Christian fortitude, springing out of Christian faith.

The lesson which we draw from the contrast is not merely that S. Paul's was a hopeful mind, and Jacob's a desponding one, though this may have been so, but that S. Paul's life was lived on a higher level than Jacob's.  And he who would be free from anxiety, and show himself superior to circumstance, must live the life that is lived with Christ in God.  Only thus can we soar above the world, and meet with a brave heart the trials which may threaten us.

Some men's lives are made both useless and miserable by their fears and forebodings.  They constantly anticipate evils which never come. They are always misjudging the future.  How futile this is !  For our fears will not ward off the blow when it descends, or avert calamity if it overtakes us.  Besides, the events which have brought us the greatest good have often been those which we most dreaded.

How mistaken was Jacob when he said, "All these things are against me!" Why! the very things which so troubled him, those same events, at the prospect of which he was so crushed and dismayed, were at that moment reshaping themselves in the hand of Providence in order to crown him with honour and blessing. Joseph and Simeon were waiting to be restored to him. Advanced in life though the patriarch was, he was about to enter upon a new era in his career which should be brighter and happier than all that had gone before. Just when the clouds were darkest, they were on the point of dispersing, leaving his sun to set in a clear sky.

At a period when other men fail, he was entering on the most joyful, the most restful, and at the same time the most triumphant years of his life.

Instead of things being against him, they were never so much in his favour. We think of Jacob's seventeen years in Egypt as the ideal of a peaceful and successful old age. Honoured by the Egyptian Pharaoh, as the venerable parent of his ablest statesman and courtier (the far-famed Joseph), with all his children about him, a united family after years of separation, notwithstanding those dissensions amongst his sons that had been such a grief to him, and which had once well-nigh ended in bloodshed. It was like a dream. Had Jacob been told that all this would happen, that Simeon and the long-lost Joseph would be restored to him, and that he should end his days in Egypt in peace and affluence, and loaded with honours, it would have seemed more impossible than any vision of the night which vanishes with our first waking thoughts.

And yet these things actually happened, and came to pass within a few weeks from the day when in bitterness of soul, and in the greatness of his parental anxiety, he had cried, "All these things are against me."

Jacob's position, in its relation to his antecedents, and to the times in which he lived, was one of unprecedented success, uniting, in his old age, both dignity and repose. To be the patriarchal head of a chosen clan, the heir of all the promises, encircled by prophetic predictions, and shielded by the Divine Blessing, each of his twelve sons destined to become a separate tribe, and these twelve tribes a united nation, a nation in some respects the most honoured and most blessed of all the nations of the earth, and to be permitted by inspiration to foresee something of this ere his eyes closed on the world, surely it was a vision brighter even than that vouchsafed

to Moses on Pisgah, as he descried in the distance
the " sweet fields beyond the swelling flood," which
marked the Promised Land.

As a noble ship, that has safely weathered some
heavy storms on the voyage, sweeps calmly and
majestically into port, with the sun shining upon
her glistening sails ; as the full ripe sheaf is
gathered home amid harvest shouts and songs of
rejoicing ; so it was with the closing days of the
Patriarch Jacob. A halo of glory shone about
his head. The trials and sorrows which had once
beset him, like summer clouds, had passed away,
to end in a peaceful old age, crowning a life full of
days and honours. And yet the events which, at
a certain perioo of his life, were rapidly converging
to this desirable fulfilment, were the same respecting which he had cried, " All these things are
against me." What a lesson on the futility of
human fears and forebodings.

In contrast to this man, whom God dealt so
mercifully with, though he was always doubting
and dreading the future, you have S. Paul, whose
life was a constant martyrdom, and who (like his
Divine Master) had often (through the teaching
of the Holy Ghost) a distinct premonition of the
dangers and trials which awaited him. I know
he said, as he went up to Jerusalem, that "bonds
and afflictions abide me, but none of these things

H

move me." So great was his confidence in God, and so thoroughly was his mind made up to pursue the path of duty at any risk, at any cost, that deterrents could hardly be said to count with S. Paul.

The only question for him was, What was the will of Christ in the matter? When once he was satisfied of this, and of the direction in which his work lay, there was nothing further to be considered.

He did not look forward to a happy and comfortable old age, like Jacob's. He knew full well, as did S. Peter, that he would be called to suffer for the faith; that that wondrous life of his, which is one long catalogue of hardships, dangers, and privations, which reads like a very romance of suffering, must end in a violent death. Yet so confident was he of the truth of his mission, and of the blessedness of it, so assured was he of the love of Christ, and of the certainty of his reward hereafter, so transitory did the pains and sufferings of this life seem to the glories which awaited him, that he could say, " None of these things move me." " I have learned, in whatsoever state I am, therewith to be content." " I know both how to be abased, and I know how to abound. Everywhere and in all things I am instructed both to be full and to be hungry, both to abound and to suffer need. I can do all things through Christ which strengtheneth me."

My brothers! which is better, the timorous foreboding of Jacob or the confident faith of S. Paul? Surely the latter is far better, for even if in this life the worst comes to pass, if our days should be darkened with care, or shortened with affliction, such a faith will prepare us for it, and enable us to meet it bravely and hopefully, so that our adversity shall be as peaceful and as blessed as was Jacob's prosperity. So shall we be independent of this world, and the good things of this world, which vanish away.

## X.

## FIFTH SUNDAY IN LENT.

### The Discipline of Trial.

EXODUS iii, 2.

" The bush burned with fire, and the bush was not consumed."

THE first Old Testament Lesson for Passion Sunday is the vision of Moses at the burning bush.

Before the teaching of Christ, and the sufferings of Christ, had interpreted to us the meaning and the blessedness of suffering, as early as the times of the Exodus, God gave to His suffering people in Egypt this parable of the beneficent discipline of trial.

What was that strange sight which arrested the steps of Moses, as he fed his flock in the desert, beneath the shadow of Mount Horeb? What was that mysterious appearance which he turned aside to see? It was the vision of the burning bush. A picture of the suffering Church of Christ in all ages. A symbol of sanctified sorrow. " The bush burned with fire, and the bush was not consumed." The perishable shrub, burning in the fierce light of God's chastenment, represented, first of all, Israel in Egypt, the race of suffering slaves, whom the historian describes as toiling in the heated brick-fields, under the lash of their brutal taskmasters. But the marvel was not that Israel was in bondage to Pharaoh, or that the Egyptians afflicted them, but that "the more they afflicted them the more they multiplied and grew." Pharaoh's cruel edicts only served to defeat the end they had in view. The more he loaded them with tasks the stronger they became. " The bush burned with fire, and the bush was not consumed." Why was this? It was because God Himself was in the fire. His hand was in the chastisement, making it remedial, and turning the curse into a blessing.

Moses had been grieving about his brethren in Egypt. His heart was with them in their cruel bondage, as he fulfilled the long years of his exile in Midian, and fed the flock of Jethro his father-in-law. And what was Jehovah's message to Moses out of the burning bush? It was just such a message as he desired. " I know their sorrows." " I have surely seen the

affliction of My people which are in Egypt," " I
have heard their cry, . . . . and am come down
to deliver them." It is the voice of the great
Father of us all speaking out of the midst of
the fire, assuring us of His tender compassion,
His unchanging love, telling from age to age,
and generation to generation, that the object of
all earthly trial is a beneficent one. It is not
some "strange thing" which has happened to
us, but the deliberate purpose of our Father's
will. He is not ignorant of our sufferings. His
own words are, " I have seen," " I know." Though
left for a time in the furnace of affliction, He still
speaks of Israel as "My people," and adds, " I
know their sorrows," proving they were not forgotten.

My brothers! it is the message of God to the
individual saint (shall I not say also to the individual sinner), as it is His message to the universal
Church. " Hear ye the rod, and who hath appointed it." We are the disciples of a suffering
Christ, if we are disciples at all. What are the
Bible figures which represent the Church of God
on earth? They are, the boat in the storm, the ark
on the waters, the dove on the wing, the bush in
the fire. These are symbols of God's own choosing. They represent conditions of our earthly
life, and we cannot change them.

Life, however, is not all trial. There are times
when God puts us into the school of privilege.
He lavishes upon us His choicest gifts. And in
the use and enjoyment of these we may learn, if
we will, all that we really need to know. But if
we rebel, if the voice of this beneficent teacher is
disregarded, and the goodness of God is not suffered, as it was intended, to lead us to repentance, then we are put back, as it were, into the
lower school of chastisement, in order that we
may learn the first lesson more thoroughly.
This is why the mystery of pain and suffering
is written in such deep and terrible characters
upon the face of God's moral government. And
the answer to the question, "Why do sorrow
and suffering abound?" is to be found, no doubt,
in the common experience of the Psalmist, when
he said, "Before I was afflicted I went astray;
but now have I kept Thy Word."

Think how many who came to Our Lord when
He was upon earth came to Him to be healed of
some bodily infirmity. It was their sorrows and
not their sins which, in the first instance, led these
poor sufferers to Christ; and through their sorrows
He led them also to see and think about their
sins. Our Saviour was only illustrating an eternal
principle of grace when He drew these to Himself
by the bands of their own infirmities. There is a

great moral purpose in trial. As Dr. Guthrie used to say, " It is the cup in every man's sack." The cup is left with us that it may lead us to return to Him who put it in our sack, as Joseph compelled his favourite brother, Benjamin, to return again to Egypt with the rest of their company. It is a Divine stratagem of mercy to restore Christ's lost and wandering sheep, and fetch them back to the shepherd and bishop of their souls. Many a mother, suffering the pains of her sex, has asked, with Rebekah, " Why am I thus ? " The answer is, that the mystery of punishment is a part of the mystery of sin, and that for all the bitter fruits of evil, the pain and anguish and woe of suffering humanity, there is a " needs be " in the counsels of Him Whose name is Holy.

What we are so slow to perceive is the near and intimate relation that exists between sin and suffering, between pain and punishment. Moral and physical ailments are closely related, and they are connected for a wise purpose. For there is not only a judicial but also a remedial object in the connection. The writer of the Epistle to the Hebrews tells us that if we " endure chastening, God dealeth with us as with sons." These words teach us to view trial in its holiest and most blessed aspect, viz., as a test of our divine sonship, since chastisement received in a spirit of submission is here represented as one of the marks of discipleship.

God's people have always been a suffering people, and the office of faith is to look beyond the trial to the purpose of the trial.

We know, under the old Jewish dispensation, that God Who accepted the sacrifice also consumed the sacrifice, and *vice versâ*. He who sent the hour of great darkness upon the mind of Abraham in the prophetic vision of His people's humiliation in Egypt, also lighted the torch of their deliverance.

Trial is the rod of God's appointment. For it is the Saviour's own hand which plaits the five-thonged scourge with which He chastises His elect and prepares them for His service and Kingdom.

Faith has always recognised a holy and beneficent purpose in sorrow. The religious instinct in man has never failed to interpret trial as Christ interpreted it. Only His sufferings have made the message clearer to us than before. To Noah, the rainbow was the chosen symbol of fruitful sorrow. The sun shining through the storm-cloud, and refracted by the falling rain-drops, was to the patriarch a token of God's faithfulness. It spoke of mercy rejoicing against judgment, and of good coming out of evil. As the promise in the cloud it taught that every form of pain or punishment has a discipline and teaching peculiar to itself, that somehow a blessing was always wrapped up in the curse. Such was the gospel according to Noah.

To Moses, as we have seen, the burning bush was the emblem of sanctifying sorrow, a picture of the oppressed Israelites in Egypt, who, the more they were afflicted, "the more they multiplied and grew." "The bush burned with fire," yet "the bush was not consumed." Such was the gospel according to Moses.

Why is it that the greatest writers of fiction always excel in the delineation of struggling virtue or unrequited heroism, so that the most perfect characters in their books generally appear in the dim light of some sad association? Is it bitterness or misanthropy which leads them to choose such subjects for their pen, and causes them to take peculiar delight in scenes which minister pain to their heroes? Nay! it is because they feel and recognise, truly, that the triumph of failure is the greatest triumph of all. The proud march of uninterrupted success is odious, vulgar, contemptible, compared with the heroism of a thwarted life.

The power to add acre to acre and prize to prize is no claim upon our neighbour's affection or esteem. Often a man who rises in importance appears less, rather than greater, in consequence of his elevation. It is when he falls that he is nearest to us; since it is the prostrate hero whose greatness we recognise first. And the novelist, who depicts life failures with tenderness and truth, will never fail to have appreciative readers, not merely because he appeals to kindred sympathies, in ourselves, with those who suffer, but also because he appeals to a secret consciousness that there is something sacred and ennobling in trial.

We have a fruitful lesson upon this subject in the history of S. Paul's trial. We do not know what that trial was. It may have been blindness. It may have been great physical prostration, severe bodily weakness, the result, perhaps, of fever. It may have been continuous unintermittent pain. Several explanations have been put forward, but they are only hypothetical, and none of them is quite satisfactory. He calls it a "thorn," or more literally a "stake," in the flesh. "There was given to me," he says, "a stake in the flesh, the messenger of Satan, to buffet me." From this we learn that good men are tried for their own good. Though the agent employed may be Satan himself, yet the trial is permitted for the saint's own benefit. It was so with Job;

and it was so with S. Paul. For there are always two sides to every trial, a dark and a bright side. The angel of Satan is often the minister of God

In itself, trial is an evil thing, and springs from evil, either evil in ourselves, in the world, or in evil angels. But on the other hand, trials may be overruled for our good, and thus become the stepping-stones to a higher life of righteousness and true holiness. Sanctified sorrow is a gift which comes from God alone. S. James taught us this when he wrote, " Blessed is the man that endureth trial."

But we may learn a further lesson upon the use of trial from the way in which S. Paul met affliction. He took it to God in prayer. "I besought the Lord thrice, that it might depart from me." Here, we learn to take our sorrows to God Himself, Who will either remove the burden or help us to bear it. The latter is the higher discipline, and the nobler fulfilment of Christ's promised help. It was thus that S. Paul's prayer was answered. The trial itself remained, but the sting of the trial was taken away. It was answered as our Lord's prayer in the Agony was answered, not by removing the cause of suffering, but by supplying the needful strength to bear it. The apostle fully recognised this, when he penned those words of holy courage which follow the description of his conflict and its blessed termination, "Most gladly, therefore, will I rather glory in my infirmities, that the power of Christ may rest upon me." "Therefore I take pleasure in infirmities, in reproaches, in necessities, in persecutions, in distresses, for Christ's sake ; for when I am weak, then am I strong." He had learned the great lesson which the trial was intended to teach, viz., that the grace of Christ is sufficient, and that His strength is made perfect in our weakness.

Is it not the very conclusion to which our sorrows point us, but which, somehow, we so often miss ? It is the continuance of the trial which staggers us. We stumble over the difficulty, and thrust it aside, but it only seems to roll back upon us with increased weight. We wrestle and pray, and still the burden is not removed. Why ? Because all the while, Christ is teaching us by the discipline of repeated failure, that His "Grace is sufficient for us," and that His "strength is made perfect in weakness." In the words of John Henry Newman, "There is a treasury in Heaven stored with such offerings as the natural man abhors ; with sighs and tears, wounds and blood, torture and death. The Martyrs first began the contribution, and we all may follow them : all of us, for every suffering, great or little, may, like the widow's mite, be sacrificed in faith to Him who sent it. Christ gave us the words of consecration when He for an ensample said, 'Thy will be done.' Henceforth, as the apostle speaks, we may 'glory in tribulation,' as the seed of future glory. Meanwhile, let us never forget in all we suffer that, properly speaking, our own sin is the cause of it, and it is only by Christ's mercy that we are allowed to range ourselves at His side. We who are children of wrath, are made through Him children of grace ; and our pains, which are in themselves but foretastes of hell, are changed by the sprinkling of His Blood into a preparation for Heaven."*

* J. H. Newman, in " Under the Cross."

## XI.

## PALM SUNDAY.

## Opportunity.

EXODUS iv. 2.
"What is that in thine hand?"

WHEN God first appeared unto Moses at the
bush, and urged him to return to Egypt as the
ambassador of Israel's deliverance, we read that
the Jewish leader hesitated, pleading his unfitness
for so arduous and difficult an undertaking. Five
times he raises some objection, and five times the
objection is dismissed and overruled. To the
plea that his oppressed kinsmen would doubt the
credentials of his mission and authority, the
Almighty replies by a question, "What is that in
thine hand?" What was it? It was his rod or
staff, his shepherd's crook, the sign at once of his
rural calling, and the implement by which he
executed that calling in the trackless wilds of

Midian. This homely crook, however, was destined, as the staff and symbol of a higher office, to become, in the hand of Moses, a far more influential agent. Henceforth, he was to be recognised by it, as the direct representative of Jehovah, and the appointed deliverer of Israel. That rod, with which he had tended his flock in the lonely desert, was from that hour to be regarded as the sacred wand, the wonder-working staff of Moses, the Man of God, the serpent-sign of power to idolatrous Egypt, the terror of her magicians, her soldiers, and her kings. Ever after, it is known, not as the rod of Moses, but as the rod of God. At the raising of that wand (the exiled Midian shepherd's crook) the ten dreadful plagues fall upon Pharaoh and his devoted kingdom. Stretched out over the deep waters of the Red Sea, the turbulent waves part hither and thither, so as to form a dry and sheltered path for God's chosen people to pass over. With his staff, Moses strikes the rock in Horeb, and, forthwith, there issues forth a rich and plenteous stream, which follows Israel throughout all their desert wanderings. While in the engagement with Amalek, the potent sign still preserves its old significance, for Moses, seated upon the brow of a neighbouring hill, is stretching out, as before, this same wonder-working rod towards the field of battle, with his two assistants, Aaron and Hur, one on either side, bearing up his wearied arms through the long day, and when the rod is uplifted, Israel has the advantage, and when it is laid down, Amalek prevails.

My brothers! I can conceive of no more striking and impressive parable for enforcing the duty of employing whatever talent or opportunity we at present possess, than this unfolded to us in the history of Moses' rod. If, like Moses, we take that which is in our hand, and use it in the name and strength of Christ our Master, if we seize the present opportunity, and make the most of that particular duty or privilege which lies nearest to us, then, we may be sure that God will be with us, as He was with Moses ; and we shall find that other duties and privileges will open out of this which we have welcomed and employed. Thus, we shall prove for ourselves, that the homely crook, whatever shape it takes, whether it be the author's pen, or the artist's pencil, the builder's rule, or the carpenter's hammer, if lifted in faith, and used with diligence, shall become, in the hand of its conscientious employer, the sign and instrument of a wonder-working power, a usefulness only divine.

Over the clock of the parish church of Knaresborough, in Yorkshire, are inscribed these words :

I

"Redeeming the time." Each movement of the finger on the dial-plate which chronicles the hours, as they come and go, points to the motto which encircles it, and reminds us that these fleeting moments (of which we are disposed to take so little count) which are silently and stealthily measuring out the pulses of our natural life, constitute, at the same time, the opportunity which is given, once at least, to every man, for acquiring earnestness of purpose and nobility of soul.

Suggestive and impressive as these words of S. Paul are, as we find them in our English translation of the Bible, they fall short of the original meaning of the text. This should be, not "redeeming the time," but "buying up," or "buying out the opportunity." The figure employed by the apostle, is that of an open market or bazaar, thronged with eager purchasers, each intent upon obtaining some rare and valued commodity, of which only a few samples are on sale. Under such circumstances it all depends upon the alertness of the buyer, to secure an early purchase. This is what the apostle means by "buying up," or "buying out the opportunity." But the word itself provides us with a further illustration. It is derived from two Latin words, "ob" and "portus," at, or before, the harbour. Suppose you were looking down from some rocky prominence upon a rough and stormy sea, and, close to the harbour wall, you were to note some trading vessel, returning from a long and prosperous voyage, just entering the home port, and making for the calm sheltered bay within the breakwater, that, in the imagery of the word itself, would represent "an opportunity"; while the neglect of opportunity would be represented by this same vessel drifting carelessly past the harbour's mouth, or standing out again to open sea, with the cruel waves sweeping her sides and breaking over her deck, just when she might have been lying peacefully at anchor, in a place of safety. Thus from the etymology of the word "opportunity" we are reminded that it depends very much upon our own care and diligence whether we shall secure the privileges held out to us in the voyage of life, or let them go.

Who can say what each of us might not have been, or have done, but for lost opportunities? I question whether there is any single feature of our past more sad to look back upon than this· There may be particular sins, which start into guilty prominence, as memory turns over the forgotten pages of our history, and conjures up fleeting images of former days; but it is not these which trouble us most, but that endless chain of forfeited privileges and lost opportunities, which

form for so many of us an almost continuous
record of the lengthening years. Childhood,
youth, and manhood, all repeat the same story,
and accuse us of the same neglect. The roll of
life is filled with blanks, where we should have
made our mark.

In every town, in every village, there are men
who ought to have been leaders, who should have
come to the front, and been foremost in the race
of life, whom we have passed and left behind,
because they were loiterers by the way, unmindful
of their calling, neglectful of their gifts.

It has often been remarked that the opportunities of famous men are rarely commensurate with
their achievements. In other words, that success
is traceable, not to the greatness of their privileges,
but to the good use which they made of those
privileges. For example, Esau had better chances
than Jacob. Pharaoh had similar advantages, and
a similar training, to Moses. Saul had the start
of David, in the occupation of the throne of Israel,
and in the affections of his people. The Jewish
priests (in the days of Herod) had more light than
the three eastern sages, who followed the star,
and presented their gifts to the infant Saviour.
But they made a poor use of their opportunities.
They were, in consequence, the victims of their
own neglect.

It is so with ourselves. In the frailties and weaknesses of the present, we reap the fruits of former negligence in years gone by. As our own Christian poet, Keble, writes :—

" And daily as we downward glide,
   Life's ebbing stream on either side
   Shows at each turn some mould'ring hope or joy,
   The Man seems following still the funeral of the Boy."

My brothers ! I do not wish to lead you to indulge in a habit of vain and useless regrets ; but sometimes it is well to glance at past omissions in order to avoid future mistakes. Such a review has a tendency to quicken our steps in the present, and lead us to greater vigilance in the future, lest we should be tempted to let the day of opportunity slip.

Already the shadows of life are lengthening "The time is short." "See then that ye walk circumspectly, not as fools, but as wise, redeeming the time, because the days are evil."

What we all need is, first, a readiness to perceive an opportunity when it is presented to us, and secondly, a determination (like that of the soldier who stands at attention) promptly to seize and make the most of the occasion for our own or our neighbour's good.

People often complain that they have no

opportunities of witnessing for Christ, and working for God in the world. They are perfectly sincere in the statement, and urge the complaint not by way of excuse but from lack of confidence in their own power or ability to influence others.

My brothers! it is a great mistake. The answer to Moses' diffidence was the question of the text, "What is that in thine hand?"

Let me ask, then, what use are we making of such privileges as we at present possess? With regard to our social relations, are we exercising the influence of Christian laymen? In our business, or our pleasures, are we witnessing for Christ in the world? Do we act from conviction, not from impulse or custom? Are we like Joseph in Egypt, or Daniel in Babylon, or Esther at the court of Ahasuerus? These were but slaves, living in heathen lands, yet they exercised a most potent influence for God and their people in the countries to which they were banished· What of our educational advantages? Is our superior education likely to prove a blessing or a curse to us? Does it lead us, as all knowledge should lead, up to the throne of God? Do we follow our star, or does the gift, like that vouchsafed to the Jewish priests of old, lead only to doubt and scepticism? Think of our religious privileges. How many and great these are compared with those enjoyed by our fore-fathers. We have not only our English Bible and our English Church, but we have inspiring services, frequent Communions, and a religious literature suited to the needs and capabilities of every age and class. These are God's helps for the strengthening and refreshing of our souls. What use are we making of these things? Few of us value our privileges as we should, until the clock strikes the hour of change, and we are called to part with them.

But again, "What is that in thine hand?" It is a gift, a talent, an opportunity. Are you wealthy? then use your money in the service of Christ, and for the good of His Church. Have you influence? then see that you exert your influence in the world on the side of virtue and religion. Is it strength that you possess? then you are called to be one of God's workers, to take the labouring oar through life as you urge your convictions against the stream of adverse criticism or supercilious indifference.

Understand, I do not assert that all men have the same opportunities, or that yours are of the highest order; but I do say that no man, however humble his position or calling in life, is destitute of opportunities for doing good. Remember, the issues of a battle depend, not only upon the courage and genius of the officers in command, but also upon the bravery of the troops.

The world will never be reformed solely by the ministrations of the clergy, or the decrees of the State, but by the co-operation of individuals acting each in his own sphere of influence, until the whole tone of society is elevated and improved. The clergy, no doubt, give an impulse to public opinion. They light a torch which others may carry. But it must be left to the laity themselves to deepen and extend the influence thus generated. For each class of society is leavened chiefly from within. A man in one station of life has but little personal influence over those in another station of life. The poor must help the poor: the rich must help the rich. If you were a clergyman, or a member of parliament, the opportunities of an ordinary citizen would be yours no longer. My brothers! your power lies in a consecrated purpose and a dedicated life, in the beauty of a holy faith, and the force of a consistent example.

"What is that in thine hand?" It is a mission, an opportunity. Why! every calling or relation in life opens out some fresh duty, some further privilege, which is associated with that particular vocation and with no other. Only think what employers of labour might do for the benefit of those who work on their farms, or in their shops, if they clearly recognised that they had higher duties to perform in connection with their "hands" than are included in the mere act of paying their wages, and providing them with regular employment. Or think, what servants who live together as partners in the same house might do in the way of mutual sympathy and help. People think that writing and preaching are the sum and substance of Christian usefulness, and that if a man is religious he must needs be a clergyman. My friends! there is no greater mistake. I am not sure whether the greatest theological book ever written could not be well exchanged for one truly self-devoted life, such as that of an Athanasius, a Luther, or a Selwyn.

It is these "living epistles" that we want. Men are wearied of religious treatises and sermons. To be convinced, they must see godliness in the life. I believe that if all our religious literature could be exchanged, book by book, for just so many noble Christian lives, that the Church and the world would be both gainers thereby.

Here, then, is our opportunity. We cannot all write books, or preach sermons in defence of the faith ; but we can live godly lives in Christ Jesus : and of this kind of literature there is a great dearth in the world.

You may remember, that at the rebuilding of the wall of Jerusalem, under Nehemiah, it is said that each repaired the breach " over against his own house." That is the principle on which we should go to work in all our projected reforms. First, begin with yourself, your own heart, your own life, your own home. Oh ! if everyone would do this, would repair the breach nearest his own door, would take the opportunity which comes first to hand, and devote his chief care and attention to that, how real and thorough would our work be ; we should be sure at any rate of securing one genuine reformation.

My brothers ! it is the witness of *lives* which the Church wants ; and it is a form of testimony which everyone can give. It comes within the reach of all.

Here, then, is a practical exposition of those words of the great apostle which each of us can apply for himself. This is, to " redeem the time," from the evil within and the evil without. This is to " buy up the opportunity."

## XII.

### GOOD FRIDAY.

#### The Sacrifice of Isaac and the Sacrifice of Christ.

GENESIS xxii. 7.

"Behold the fire and the wood ; but where is the lamb for a burnt offering ?"

THE first Lesson for this morning's service sets before us the sacrifice of Isaac as the Old Testament teaching for Good Friday.

We always speak of the *sacrifice* of Isaac, yet that sacrifice was consummated only in a figure. As an offering of will, both in the persons of the father and the son, it was a sacrifice real enough, and God accepted the will for the deed. Similarly we speak of our Lord's sacrifice, before its actual fulfilment on the Cross, as having already taken place. He was "the Lamb slain from the foundation of the world," always slain, always dedicated, in the Divine intention, consecrated and accepted, through the eternal will of Him to Whom past, present, and future are alike one.

Again, in the case of Isaac, the actual and literal sacrifice was by deputy, since God provided a substitute for the willing victim. And although in the Great Sacrifice there was no substitute, for Christ Himself " bare our sins in His own body on the tree," yet what happened on Mount Moriah may serve to image for us two truths.

One is, that Christ, the Eternal Sacrifice, was the true and veritable substitute for every repentant sinner, who, through his own personal contrition (as a willing offering) has nailed his sins to the Cross.

And beyond this, in the Great Sacrifice, there is a still further application of the principle and idea of substitution. For in the sacrifice of Christ it was not an individual man only that suffered, but the racial, representative, universal Man. As such, we understand, Christ died " once " for all men, for the whole race, and not for a few members of that race.

To a certain class of mind the sacrifice of Isaac offers grounds for criticism. There are always some who find it easy to suggest difficulties and construct objections to Holy Writ. " Why," they will say, " did God ask this thing ? " " Can the

good God tempt? How could a righteous man
obey so sanguinary a command? If the steel of
Abraham's character was so finely tempered, why
then did he not perceive that human sacrifice was
itself immoral, and repugnant alike both to God
and man?"

To myself, I confess, such questions appear
impertinent, rather than important. They hardly
deserve an answer. They are as out of place as a
coarse joke beside an open grave; and are as far
beneath the spirit of Abraham's faith and Isaac's
obedience as the question of the Sadducees
respecting a resurrection was beneath the teaching of Christ. To those, however, who honestly
feel the difficulties to which I have referred, it
may be said, in the words of the Bishop of
London: "We must not expect to find the
ideas or the morality of later times in early
ages."

We have repeated examples in history of the
noblest minds being warped and blinded by the
influence of traditional usage or the want of
knowledge and training. It should be remem-
bered, too, that throughout the whole story there
are indications that Abraham looked for some
Divine interposition, which should provide a
way of escape from what he both dreaded and
abhorred. At the same time it must be conceded

that, from his widely different standpoint and
environment, the patriarch was unable, as we
are, to regard the act as intrinsically immoral ;
and his deep religious sense invested a rite, in
itself revolting and horrible, with attributes of a
high spiritual order. For in the mind of
Abraham the offering was idealised, and was
regarded as an act of pure worship, in the homage
of the affections and the sacrifice of self ; an
act, too, of perfect and absolute renunciation, in
obedience to the will of God.

Once satisfied that this awful demand represented the path of duty, it seemed to the patriarch
clear and unmistakable that he must yield to it a
literal and unquestioning obedience, and leave the
result to God.

In what way the Almighty would accomplish
His purpose, vindicate His honour, and deliver
His servant, Abraham was not informed. From
a passage in the Epistle to the Hebrews, it
would seem that in his agony and perplexity,
through the intense light which strong feeling
sometimes casts upon a subject, he received a
clear and definite intimation of the hidden truth
of " a resurrection, even from the dead ; " and
from a sentence of Our Lord we gather, that
in some way it was revealed to the patriarch
that the sacrifice of his son was intended to

convey a great spiritual lesson. In other words, that there was attached to it some mystic meaning, hidden in the purpose of God, concerning the ultimate fulfilment, both of the idea and the need of sacrifice. "Your father Abraham rejoiced to see My day ; and he saw it and was glad."

We are accustomed to think of Abraham as the brave pioneer, the 'hardy emigrant, the man who, at the call of God, left his primeval home, in the distant East, to commence the march, and direct the tide of westward emigration, which has been flowing on ever since. We think of his massive independence, his commercial acumen, his parental authority, ruling his family and dependents with a firm and righteous discipline. But we must not forget that the patriarch's migration was in obedience to the call of God. It was an act of faith. The same faith which led him, wherever he went, to rear, in simple devotion, an altar for the worship of the Most High ; a faith so strong, so wonderful, that it staggered not at the promise, nor faltered, even when that promise was so long delayed, that its Divine fulfilment seemed impossible. Nor should we lose sight of the tenderness which is often associated with firmness in truly great men. We see it in the parting with Hagar, as he put the water-bottle on the shoulder of the weeping girl ; in the prayer for Ishmael and the intercession for Sodom. We see it in his dealings with Ephron, the Hittite, when the grand old chieftain stood up from before his dead, to purchase that mournful plot, the only spot he ever possessed in the land of Canaan, as a burial-place for Sarah, his wife. Above all, we see it in the stern suppression of all outward feeling, in the preparation for the sacrifice of "his son, his only son."

Thus, in the character of Abraham we find independence, dignity, uprightness of a high order, and what is even less common, faith, unconquerable faith, proving itself in the surrender of all that was dearest, reaching to the very crown and climax of self-sacrifice, in the relinquishment of what had been the inspiring hope and ruling desire of a lifetime.

To every call of God, whether in the direction of service or suffering, the answer of Abraham was always, "Here am I, Lord, here am I." And so in ready response, as though he set about some pleasant task, the torturing decision was made, and the trying journey commenced, which was to end, as it seemed to the stricken father, in an irretrievable loss. For "Abraham rose up early in the morning," we are told, "and saddled his ass, and took two of his young men with him, and Isaac, his son, and clave the wood for the burnt-offering, and rose up, and went unto the place of which God had told him. Then, on the third day, Abraham lifted up his eyes, and saw the place afar off." What a prospect! how the sight must have struck a chill to the heart of this sorrowful father as the journey neared its fulfilment. The distant peak of Mount Moriah,[1] as it came first into view, must have added greatly to the patriarch's realisation of the terrible renunciation required in the awful sacrifice of his son. What before had been a vague and undefined dread would immediately take definite shape in the actual scene of its threatened enactment. But, like our Blessed Lord on His last visit to Jerusalem, with His Cross full in view, Abraham did not halt or waver as the destined goal appeared above the horizon, a material evidence of the trial which awaited him.

Well! this illuminating vision of the Cross, this appearance of Mount Moriah on the horizon of our life, may have a counterpart in our own personal experience.

For example, at a certain point in our history health fails, a child sickens, or a business declines. We refuse, however, to think the matter serious, or at any rate imminent. We regard it only as a gloomy foreboding, a passing cloud. But one

[1] Probably " Gerizim," Stanley's " Jewish Church."

day the doctor's verdict, or the year's balance sheet, confirms the unwelcome suspicion, and precludes all possibility of mistake or postponement. Moriah rises into view, and as it stands out in clear and ominous outline against the threatening sky, we know that we must ourselves face the cross, and bear it to its destined end.

At any rate, the experience of Abraham is one which, in some form, or in some degree, we must one day share. Every incident in the narrative is suggestive and touching in the extreme. The whole story is instinct with tender pathos and beautiful feeling. For example, in the instruction given to the attendants left behind at the point reached on the third day of the journey, "Abide ye here with the ass; and I and the lad will go yonder and worship, and come again to you"; how the father's grief is merged and swallowed up in the saint's assurance that what God wills is best, "Shall not the judge of all the earth do right?" Similarly, the pain of renunciation is all but forgotten in the instinct of worship, which reaches above all forms or modes of expression (however dignified or however unworthy), to the end of all faith and all sacrifice, viz., communion with God, Himself: "I and the lad will go yonder and worship." What a service! What an offering!

How unworthy do our fasts or our Communions appear by comparison with this magnanimous act of self-surrender and self-sacrifice ! " I and the lad will go yonder and worship." And when we think of the degradation involved in the one offering, and the privileges offered in the other, the contrast is emphasised still more.

In the words of a great preacher, " Old Testament history gives us more than one glimpse of a pair of kindred souls, walking side by side on a journey with vast issues, knowing that they must soon say farewell, and dreading unspeakably the moment of saying it." The journey to Mount Moriah is one of them. " Here father and son  .  .  .  .  are walking side by side, and the mystery of an awful secret divides them. Was there ever journey like that journey ; ever a trial like that which, as with the piercing of a sword, searched Abraham ?  .  .  .  The very sight of the son, who so absolutely trusted him with an unsuspecting love,  .  .  .  .  must have stirred in his heart an untold anguish."[1] The lad's own question, too, " Behold the fire and the wood ; but where is the lamb for a burnt offering ?" how it must have wrung the father's heart thus to be questioned respecting what seemed the inevitable sacrifice ! How the

[1] Bishop Thorold, " The Gospel of Work."

astonished pleading of the innocent victim must have added to the torture of that astounding renunciation !

Everything seemed destined to try the faith and fortitude of this brave and tender old man.  Just when his hopes had ripened in fulfilment there came this strange incomprehensible demand, with its uncompromising condition that the patriarch's own hand should unsheath the sacrificial knife, and present, in one superlative offering, the embodiment of his most cherished aspirations. And so great was his faith in God that the demand was neither questioned nor denied.  With an alacrity, which had all the spontaneity of a free choice, he laid, upon the flaming altar of duty, the quivering flesh of a purely natural affection. The early start, the three days' journey, the toiling ascent of Mount Moriah (as father and son together climb the rugged steep, whose crest was to witness the climax of the great renunciation), all attest the heroic faith and steadfast purpose of this ideal worshipper, this spiritual chieftain, this father of the Universal Church.

And the scene itself, how shall we describe it ? A lone and dreary mountain-top, desolate and bare, isolated from all human associations, fit image of the loneliness of death, yet inspiring in its outlook, and elevating in its complete detachment from any earthly interests, with a nearness to the Infinite, unattainable, incomprehensible, amid surroundings less impressive and sublime. With such an environment, the solitary nature of the offering (only the principal actors themselves employed) appears at once both fitting and inevitable. For, as the Saviour's person was veiled and protected during His last conflict by the preternatural darkness which enveloped the Cross, so, at the sacrifice on Mount Moriah no intruding presence was permitted to break the silence, or detract from the solemnity, of that sacred mysterious rite.

Or think of the careful ordering of the simple ritual as Abraham reared an altar, and laid upon it the emblematic wood for the impending offering, binding his son Isaac, and laying him " on the altar upon the wood." How suggestive, too, the fact that the elements of destruction were provided by the victim himself, who bare up the rugged steep, the fiery elemental cross, the material necessary to consume the sacrifice.

What a parable is here! The obedience of the son, equalled only by the faith and steadfastness of the father. Their joint participation in the offering, twice emphasized, " And they went both of them together."

My brothers! if Abraham were enabled to

L

apprehend, through the gift of inspiration and the illuminating power of trial, something of the divine purpose and the divine fulfilment of sacrifice, if he was permitted to see the day of Christ, and to look forward to the one and only offering, presented on Calvary, still more do we, who have received the message of the Cross, look back to the earlier offering on Mount Moriah as the first Passion Play, the first rehearsal and representation of that which was to follow.  To us Abraham's renunciation and Isaac's obedience are living parables of that divine act which we commemorate to-day.  May that precious blood-shedding be often in our thoughts!  As we hold the Cross before our eyes, may it be to us the very gospel of reconciliation, our hope in life, our confidence in death.  May we never forget that what Abraham essayed to do, that the Eternal Father actually did, when " He spared not His Own Son, but delivered Him up for us all."  In the power of that death (which is imaged in every Baptism and rehearsed in every Communion) we defy death.  In memory of that sacrifice we keep our Good Friday.  In the spirit of that sacrifice we learn to suffer and endure.  By faith in that sacrifice we fight the good fight, and contend, earnestly, for the truths once delivered to the saints.  In the merits of that sacrifice we offer not only our prayers and praises to God, but "we present ourselves" also, "our souls and bodies," a living sacrifice to Him Who died for us. "O Saviour of the world, Who by Thy Cross and Precious Blood hast redeemed us, Save us, and help us, we humbly beseech Thee, O Lord."— (Office for the Visitation of the Sick, Book of Common Prayer.)

# XIII.

## EASTER DAY.

### Life Restored and Amplified.

JOHN xi. 25, 26. (R.V.)

"Jesus said . . . I am the resurrection, and the life: he that believeth on Me, though he die, yet shall he live; and whosoever liveth and believeth on Me shall never die."

For nineteen hundred years the Church of Christ has expressed her belief in the doctrine of a Resurrection. For nineteen hundred years, on the strength of that belief, she has uttered words of hope over the graves of the departed. Year after year, decade after decade, century after century, we have carried our loved ones to their last resting-place, in the same pious confidence, and buried our dead out of our sight. Yet we see no fruit of that sowing. Generation has followed generation; nations have lived and grown old and passed away. Empires and dynasties and states have fallen and crumbled into decay. Some have even succeeded to a temporary resurrection, as regards their social and political life, and have risen again to power and opulence under new governments, new legislators, and new laws ; but the dead still sleep their unbroken sleep, and the earth refuses to give back her spoils. Yet the Church, with unwearied faith (as she repeats, week by week, the old Creeds), continues to declare, with unabated confidence, Her unwavering belief in "the Resurrection of the dead, and the life of the World to come."

Let us this glad Easter Morning look a little more closely into the hope expressed in these words. Not that we can explain the mystery of a Resurrection ; that mystery is bound up with the mystery of life itself. The marvel in either case is the same. The difficulty is neither greater nor less in the one case than in the other. When we can understand *creation*, we may expect to comprehend *resurrection*. But at present, we must be content to leave the subject where S. Paul leaves it : "Behold, I show you a mystery." It is a matter of revelation. "The dead shall be raised incorruptible, and we shall be changed." "Marvel not at this," says our blessed Lord, for "the hour is coming, and now is, when the dead shall hear the voice of the Son of God :

and they that hear shall live." Here is the
promise of Scripture. And this promise is further
substantiated by an historical fact, viz., the fact
that Christ is risen. Out of these two things, a
Divine promise, and an historical fact, springs our
belief in a Resurrection. On these two pillars, the
arch is formed which spans both worlds.

The doctrine of a Resurrection. then, is still
matter of faith with us, not of knowledge. Yet,
on no single doctrine of revelation has faith more
conclusive evidence to rest upon. And here, let
me say, that it may assist us to clearer views, and
a deeper faith in this doctrine to regard the
Resurrection as the natural accomplishment of
what Christ our Saviour came on earth to do, and
all the miracles which Jesus did during His three
years' ministry, as so many fragments of that
same work, hints, as it were, by the way, of the
blessed purpose which He had in view: so many
partial manifestations of His glory, and of the
final work of Redemption. For, with some two
exceptions, intended as warnings to the im-
penitent, all the Christian miracles had a similar
object, and contained a common principle ; since
they were either *restorations* or *amplifications* of
nature. Thus, Jesus gave sight to the blind, He
healed the leper, He unstopped the ears of the
deaf, He gave strength to palsied limbs ; He

raised the dead in every age and stage of dissolution. Each of these acts was a restoration of some natural gift or power. Thus, Christ has taught us what was the nature of His work on earth. It was to restore to men their forfeited powers.

But some of our Lord's miracles were *amplifications* rather than mere restorations of nature. They point to a higher use, and a nobler employment of our present gifts and faculties. The stater, lying useless in the fish's mouth, Christ dedicates to a holy service. He turns water into wine and multiplies the loaves to feed the starving multitudes. And what was this but doing in part, step by step, and little by little, what our Resurrection will secure to us as a whole. For, it will not only restore to us those powers which we have lost, which have been in abeyance because maimed and crippled by sin, but it will also amplify those powers by greatly adding to their expansion and development. It seems to me most instructive and helpful to view the Christian miracles in this light, as tokens and evidences of the recuperative work of Redemption. They suggest to us the true nature of our Saviour's mission. They form a progressive series of short lessons upon the final work of Redemption, in the " Resurrection of the dead, and the life of the world to come." Here, nature will be both restored and amplified; according to that true saying, " I am come that they might have life, and that they might have it more abundantly."

It is true that we do not know the conditions of that nobler and more amplified life, but we know that to those who have been faithful in little, opportunity will be given to be faithful also in much. We are sure that the intelligence of that life will be of a far higher order than now, and that scope will be given for the prosecution of human activities on a far grander scale than is possible to us in this world.

We speak of freedom of thought and freedom of action, but this freedom is seldom realised on earth. There, however, with purified hearts and emancipated powers, our wish may be consummated. What is speech, what is friendship, what is worship, even, on earth, but a poor endeavour to fulfil those deeper instincts after communion with God and man, which we all feel and recognise? But *there*, the obstacles and hindrances to this communion which now beset us will be removed, and in the fuller, freer life of the Resurrection state, we shall find expression for our deepest affections and our noblest powers.

We read in the Gospel of S. Luke, at the raising of the widow's son, when our Lord had stopped the bier, and called to life the silent dead, that " He gave him to his mother"; the widow's only son who had left her. That was exquisite joy to the loving, compassionate heart of Jesus, our Saviour. And one day that scene will be re-enacted on a scale of infinite grandeur, when the faithful dead shall be summoned, each from his solitary tomb, to be presented alive among the company of the blessed and glorified saints. Then shall Christ our Saviour once more give children to their parents, and parents to their children, and join again the parted hands of relatives and friends, as He brings forth those whom He has safely kept under the nestling wings, and beneath the sheltering and preserving care of His unchanging love. Not one shall be missing in that day of all who died in the faith and fear of their Redeemer, Christ; while to the bliss of the Resurrection birth shall be added the joy of a blessed re-union, in the perfected fellow-ship of the Saints, in glory everlasting.

# EASTER DAY.

## XIV.

### The Fact and Hope of Easter.

ACTS iv. 2.

"They taught the people, and preached through Jesus the resurrection from the dead."

S. PAUL has elsewhere shown at some length, that our belief in a Resurrection must rest on our belief in the Resurrection of our Lord Jesus Christ. And the same connection is here alluded to in the text. They preached through the historical fact of our Saviour's Resurrection the doctrine of a general Resurrection. The Resurrection of Jesus, then, is the foundation upon which all our hopes are based, for, as the apostle says, "If Christ be not risen, then is our preaching vain, and your faith is also vain." The work of prophet and apostle, of martyr and evangelist is undone ; the whole Church of Christ is disestablished ; the whole

fabric of Christianity must crumble into dust.
Pull down your churches, sweep out your pulpits,
dismiss your clergy, bury your Bibles; for, if
Christ be not risen, revelation has no message,
and Christianity no gospel for mankind. "Then
they also which are fallen asleep in Christ are
perished." Talk not of sacred dust and consecrated ground, for if Christ be not risen, there
*is* no Resurrection of the dead, and those whom
we have buried in hope, are lost in oblivion.
This life is then the whole of man, and death
is the end of him.

Why do we bury our dead with religious
solemnities? Why do we carry them so carefully
to their last sleeping-place, and cover their
graves with flowers? Why do we set apart
churchyards and cemeteries for this sacred deposit,
and call them "God's acre"? Why do we tread
so softly over those green mounds which mark
the place where the departed lie? Why do we
treat a corpse as a sacred thing? It may be
the relic of one we have thought little of in
life, but we honour it in death. It may be
Lazarus who died in poverty at Dives' gate,
or Absalom who died in infamy in the wood
of Ephraim. No matter! We still treat their
remains with respect, for we feel that those
remains are holy. Do you ask me, why we

do such things? I answer, it is because nineteen hundred years ago, a man in Eastern
Palestine, Who poured out his life on a Roman
gibbet as a common malefactor, not only died
as other men die, but also rose again, as other
men shall one day rise. And, if you ask,
why then did people treat their dead with
respect even before Christ rose? I answer,
because the hope of that Resurrection had
preceded the act of Resurrection itself. And
this is why we carry our loved ones to the
grave, and sing hymns at their interment; and
console ourselves with farewell looks (as for
a time only), because we bury them "in sure
and certain hope" of a joyful Resurrection.
And this is why we honour our churchyards
and cemeteries, because we feel that these gardens
of death will one day bloom and bear fruit in
a life beyond the grave. This hope, which man
has ever held (a hope which neither Time nor
Death could quench or silence) has been con-
firmed by the actual Resurrection of Jesus, our
Lord, from the dead. For that Resurrection
teaches us two things :—

First, that life is not extinguished at death.

Second, that the body will be associated with
the soul in the life to come.

And first, the Resurrection of Jesus proves to

us that life is not extinguished at death, for
though the Scriptures might teach this, and though
we might believe it, yet we should have had no
proof of it, but for the Resurrection of Jesus Christ.
But His rising from the tomb in the actual body of
His flesh gave indisputable proof that the life of
man may be continued after death. Human life
is often represented as a shattered column, a
broken shaft ; and as a mere emblem of our
mortality (regarding this life only) the figure is
true enough. But it is not true, if we look beyond
the grave. For, hereafter, the broken shaft will be
restored, and stand erect in the strength and
symmetry of a renewed and perfected life.

But the Resurrection of our Lord not only
proves that the soul may exist after death, but
shows also that it will be associated with a body
in the life to come. It is this that some men
find so hard to believe. But what was possible
for one is possible for another. And if there
is anything certain about the Lord Jesus, it
is that He rose from the dead in a body, which
though it was transformed, and differed in some
important respects from the body in which He
had lived and died on earth, was yet in all essential
particulars the same body in which He was
crucified. To speak quite accurately, there was
*identity* between the natural body in which Christ

died, and the spiritual body in which He rose. And this is all for which S. Paul or any Christian teacher or apologist contends. No one desires to assert that the future body after death is the same in its powers or conditions as the body of this present life. Those conditions will, no doubt, be much changed, and those powers greatly extended. It was the mistake which the Sadducees made when they brought to the Saviour, as they thought, an unanswerable difficulty in the case of an imaginary family of seven brothers, who, dying one by one, and succeeding to the position and responsibilities of their deceased brothers, were, according to Jewish custom, all in turn married to one wife. If there was a Resurrection, they argued, each of the seven could then claim this woman as his wife. The whole difficulty, you observe, is based upon the unworthy and un-necessary assumption that the conditions of the heavenly state remain the same as in this world ; whereas our Lord distinctly asserts that the conditions hereafter are changed ; and that the relations of *that* life, however much they may resemble this, and retain the memory of our present state on earth, are infinitely nobler and freer, and are, moreover, varied in some important particulars. Hence the Sadducees' difficulty drops to pieces of itself, and quickly falls to the ground, when their false assumption is disposed of. "Ye do greatly err," said our Lord, in answer to them ; "for in the Resurrection they neither marry, nor are given in marriage, but are as the angels of God in heaven." "Ye therefore do greatly err, because ye know not the Scriptures, neither the power of God."

Again, no one has a right to assert that the future body of the Resurrection is the same in all its material elements as the body of our flesh. Both Scripture and reason are against such a position. All that we claim is, that the two shall have *identity*. It may be, that as trial and pain are necessary to purify the soul from evil, so, in like manner, death itself is necessary to purge our material nature from its grosser and more earthly elements, and that which to us is so revolting now, viz., the disintegration of the body, and the perishing of those features upon which the image of God has been stamped, is in truth only the submission of what is mortal to Nature's furnace for the purifying of that image from all that is unworthy, in order that the spiritual body, reinvested with nobler and more amplified powers, may at last become a meet companion of the emancipated spirit, a casket, fitted to contain the jewel of the soul in the day when "Mortality shall be swallowed up of Life."

Those bright spring flowers with which we
decorate our churches at Eastertide, which are
emblems of Nature's annual Resurrection, have
they not been growing silently through the dark
days of winter, before they were clothed with
their present form and beauty? Some of them
may even have been hidden away, buried beneath
the driven snow, to teach us that Death will end
in Life, as winter opens out in summer; that
as surely as night comes before day, so "they
that sow in tears shall reap in joy." First, "that
which is natural, and afterward that which is
spiritual." First the fruit of sin, the pain and
strife of dying, the long separation, the anguish of
parting, and then the joy of reunion, when
"Death is swallowed up in victory."

"I have set before thee an open door," is the
promise of Him Who has "the keys of Hades and
of Death." That promise, it is true, has a more
immediate application; but it will include this,
that Christ through His vacated tomb has set
before mankind an open door. Death is a prison-
house into which all must enter; a captivity
which shuts out the world, with all its varied
interests and activities, and seals the lips as with
a vow of perpetual silence. But into that prison-
house the Son of Man has entered, and returned
with the key of deliverance in His hand. And

by right of His victory over death He is able to set before us " an open door."

Men call themselves Christians, and think that they can believe on Christ for the forgiveness of sins and yet dispense with this doctrine of a Resurrection. They imagine that it is only an isolated point in the Christian system, a single and detached article of belief, which they may accept or refuse as they please, but this is not so. To deny the Resurrection of Christ is to deny the Divinity of Christ, and the Atonement of Christ, the Intercession of Christ, and the Second Coming of Christ. It is to deny that we have a true and living Saviour at the right hand of God, Who is appointed to be the future Judge of men. You cannot retain your faith and hope in Christ and reject His Resurrection. The two must stand or fall together. If Christ has not risen, there is no Resurrection of the dead, hereafter ; and this life is the whole of man. Hence, there is no Saviour from sin, and no forgiveness of sin. This doctrine which you seek to expunge is not a part of your faith, an isolated branch of Christian dogma ; it is the very essence of the Christian faith, and inseparable from its reception.

Hence, it follows, that our view of life cannot fail to be elevated or depressed, according as we accept or reject this doctrine, for to the man

whose faith stops short of a belief in the Resurrection, what is life but a toilsome journey,
leading to an open grave; a prospect inexpressibly
sad? Where, I ask, is the doctrine which shall
prove our stay and comfort in the hour of trial or
bereavement? How can we expect to rise above
the discouragements of our lot without this sus-
taining hope? If it be true that all that is noblest
in life must end abruptly in that inevitable catas-
trophe which overtakes all alike, why continue
any longer the unequal contest with nature, and
with self? " Let us eat and drink ; for to-morrow
we die." Such is the inevitable conclusion to
which the pitiless logic of such a creed must
necessarily drive us. What a contrast to the view
of life entertained by S. Peter in the first chapter
of his first Epistle. How satisfied, how thankful
is that view. What quiet confidence does it
express in that distant future which, to many, is
such a vague and shadowy outlook. How clearly
was the light shining over the everlasting hills,
which streamed into the soul of the aged apostle
as the day declined and the night drew on.
" Blessed be the God and Father of our Lord
Jesus Christ, which according to His abundant
mercy hath begotten us again unto a lively hope
by the resurrection of Jesus Christ from the dead,
to an inheritance incorruptible, and undefiled, and

that fadeth not away, reserved in heaven for you, who are kept by the power of God through faith unto salvation ready to be revealed in the last time."

Oh! to be able thus to face sorrow, bereavement, or death; to have a hope such as this when called to relinquish what we most value. Happy is the man who, as years increase, and earthly friendships narrow, can still choose words such as these to express the unshaken convictions of his soul. Who would not wish to end life with a faith thus steadfast and sure? Well, the great Easter message is sounding once more in our ears. " Christ is risen from the dead, and become the first-fruits of them that are asleep." Nay, we have the words of the Master Himself to inspire us with this confidence. " Fear not; I am the first and the last: I am He that liveth, and was dead; and, behold, I am alive for evermore, Amen; and have the keys of Hades and of Death."

*Jarrold & Sons, Ltd., Printers, The Empire Press, Norwich.*